In Barbara's Words

(PLUS SOME OF WALT'S & A FEW OF ELEANOR ROOSEVELT'S)

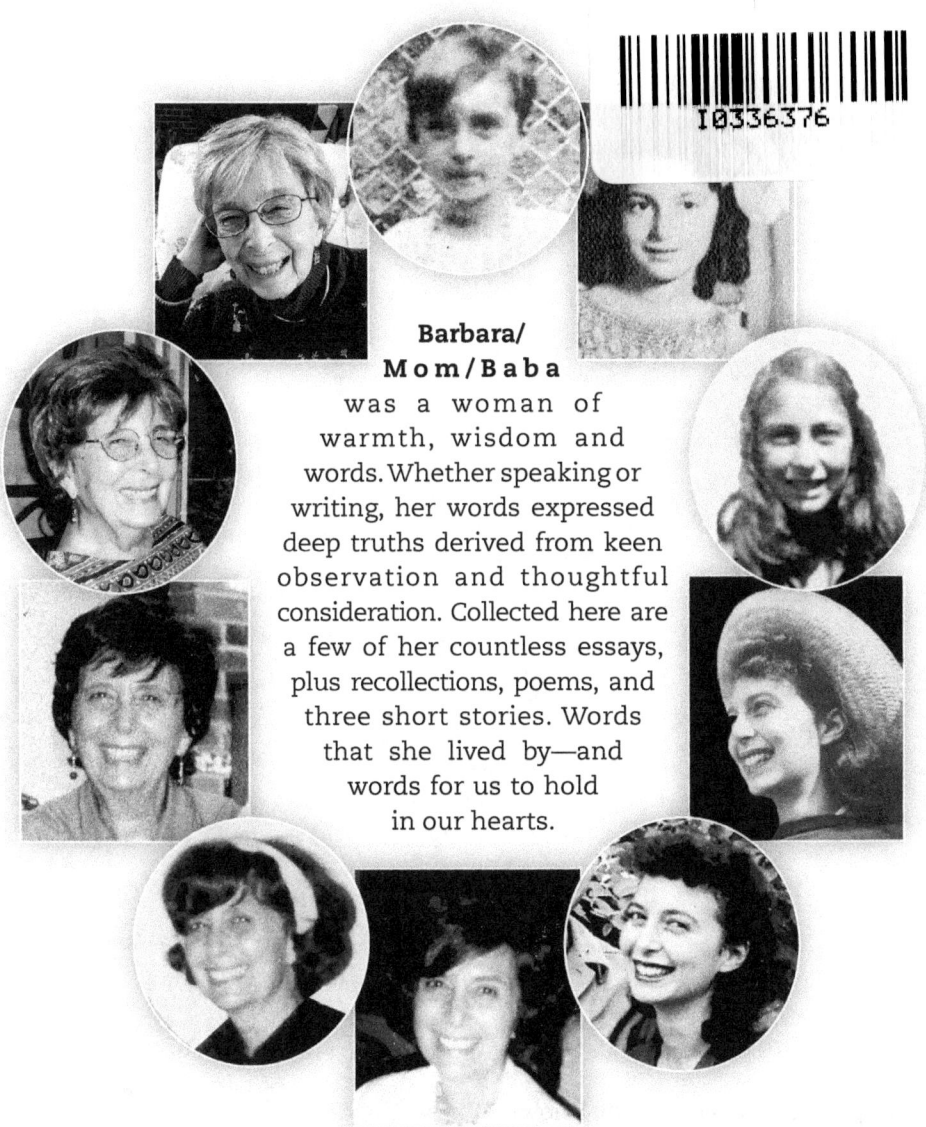

Barbara/ Mom/Baba was a woman of warmth, wisdom and words. Whether speaking or writing, her words expressed deep truths derived from keen observation and thoughtful consideration. Collected here are a few of her countless essays, plus recollections, poems, and three short stories. Words that she lived by—and words for us to hold in our hearts.

Essays, Stories & Poems by Barbara Scheiber

Compiled With Love By Her Children

In Barbara's Words: Essays, Stories & Poems by Barbara Scheiber

Copyright © 2021 by Little Known Stories
Susan Spangler, 402 Dean Dr, Rockville, MD 20851

All rights reserved.

ISBN 978-0-578-31043-5

From the Kaddish

In the rising of the sun and in its going down,
we remember her.

In the blowing of the wind and in the chill of winter,
we remember her.

In the opening of buds and in the rebirth of spring,
we remember her.

In the blueness of the sky and in the warmth of summer,
we remember her.

In the beginning of the year and when it ends,
we remember her.

When we are weary and in need of strength,
we remember her.

When we are lost and sick at heart,
we remember her.

When we have joys we yearn to share,
we remember her.

So long as we live, she too shall live,
for we remember her,
and she is a part of us.

Contents

Legacy 1

Family Stories 3
    Barbara's Childhood Memories 4
    Barbara Talks About Mollie's Family 11
    The Brisket Story 13
    Gus Scheiber's & Lillie Hellerman's Memories
        of Childhood 16
    The Scheiber Place in Putnam Valley, by Walt Scheiber 20
    Walt's Recollections 26

Essays & Articles 31
    Vassar Calls on Clarion: The Class of '42 Helps Start
        the Grassroots Offensive 32
    My Day: Three Vassar Girls Show Civilians
        How to Aid War Effort, by Eleanor Roosevelt 43
    What Kind of World Do You Want? 44
    Our Town 49
    Gift of the MRI 54
    New Windows 56
    Inaugural Vision 59
    Moving 61
    Speech to the National Association of Regional Councils 64

Jewish Holiday Stories 67
    Rosh Hashanah and Yom Kippur 68
    The Story of Hanukkah 70
    Passover 73

Poems 81
- Beginning 82
- To Write a Poem 83
- Departure 84
- Eighth Grade 86
- Divisions 88
- String 90
- Piano 94
- My Mother's Song to Her Children
  and Grandchildren 95
- View From My Kitchen Window 96
- Icicles Hanging From Our Roof 97
- January Robins 98
- To Hang an Earring 99
- Twenty Years 100
- Light 101
- In Moonlight 102
- The Stone 104
- March of the Signs 106
- Put to Sleep 111
- Daffodils 114
- On Turning 90 115
- Webs 116

Short Stories 119
- Miami Dragon 120
- Diagnosis 131
- Paradise Garden 143

Legacy

January 30, 2009

Leaving a legacy sounds like something only really important people do. But thinking about it, I imagine everyone leaves a legacy, and we all hope it will be a positive one. Is it what you hope people will remember you for? Or what you feel is the best you've tried to do, and feel proud to pass on to the younger generations? Probably a combination of many things. Here are some thoughts that come to me about what might be my own…

I think about our family itself as legacy—children, grandchildren, great-grandchildren. Loving, loyal and supportive to each other, hardworking, good—and appreciative of life. I don't claim credit for all their good qualities, but know that pieces of me are in them—pleasure in art and learning, caring for others who need them, serious pursuit of their goals, putting their ideals ahead of personal gain. There are so many pieces from so many others, but I do know I'm part of each member of the family, and that gives me joy.

That leads me to other thoughts. Our youngest child was born with a disability that affected all aspects of his development. His growth—into a self-respecting member of the community we live in—has taught me so much. The most important lesson for me is this: everyone, every individual, has the capacity to grow and learn, to feel his or her own value and ability, to enjoy life. Working with schools to get him the education he needed, learning from others how he could move forward, dealing with his problems and hurts and victories led me into writing books and articles and doing other work for people with disabilities. I hope that in some small way my work is a legacy—a firm belief that the light of potential lies in everyone, no matter how hard their problem may be—and it is our challenge and responsibility to see that light, and help to fulfill that potential.

During the last presidential campaign, our grown children and their children worked hard for Barack Obama. This made me really happy—not only because I wanted him to win, but because all my life I've been passionate about being an active citizen. It's a good feeling to see that spirit living on.

Family Stories

Barbara's Childhood Memories

Interviewed October 2007

First of all, we lived in Bronx Park South, in a basement apartment, till I was 5 years old, so that's where I was born. The story is that my grandmother, Bubbe Elke, who was a midwife, delivered me. More detail—she was present at the delivery, and she said, "If the doctor tries to use instruments, I will cut his hands off." She was obviously someone with high ideals and a strong personality. I don't know whether I remember her, but we have a picture of her holding me when I was a year old. She was there, a loving, commanding presence.

Other memories of living there, very few. I have hardly any memories of that location. But I do remember that my hair was cut in a boyish bob, very, very stylish for those days, and there's a picture of that, too, of me standing next to a wicker carriage with my mother wrapped in a fur coat. I hated it; I actually felt humiliated by it. I felt they wanted to turn me into a boy. And they just wanted me to look stylish. They. My mother.

This was true of many, many people who lived in that group at that time, who grew up on the Lower East Side of New York and began to go up in the world. Some went to Brooklyn, but most went to the Bronx. The Bronx was not fancy, but it was a step up. And from there, they went to Washington Heights. So many did it, that it seems to me to be a migratory pattern.

173rd Street, Washington Heights, is where I remember my childhood. We moved there when I was five. The first apartment was at 736 W. 173rd Street, then later, 725. They were six-story buildings, walk-ups all the way, no elevator. I think we were on the fifth floor. Also, we had a dumbwaiter, which was for carrying up the ice. We did have an icebox, but I don't remember for how long. My father thought it was very funny to say that when he came home late, he came up in the dumbwaiter. Donald and I thought that was very funny, too.

We lived opposite a park, which has so many visual memories, some good, some not so good. There was a hill that we slid down, all of us, every winter. There was a lot of snow. There was a haunted house on a hill that kept us away—a big, empty mid-Victorian house, ominous-looking. I played in the park a lot and had a lot of different people to play with. My friend Georgette Blumenthal and I made a lot of dioramas in third grade at P.S. 173. One day we were in the park, gathering some moss to make the diorama look real, and all of a sudden, a man appeared and began to run after us. We got very scared, and we ran and ran and ran, with that explosive feeling of fear. But we never talked about it to anyone.

One of the most vivid memories of my childhood during that period was the kidnapping of the Lindbergh baby. I believe that everyone of my generation who grew up in New York was haunted by that. I was always afraid of being kidnapped. There was a fire escape outside my window, and I never wanted the window to be open, because a kidnapper might come in. Also, when I would come home from school, I had to pass a lot of alleyways, and I would run very fast past them. And we were warned constantly, "Don't go anywhere with a stranger. Don't take food from a stranger. Don't get in a car." Again and again and again. It was partly because we played unsupervised on the street, so those warnings intensified after the Lindbergh kidnapping. We were on the street from the minute school was out till supper time.

It was *my* neighborhood. Every afternoon, we played hopscotch, drawing the squares on the sidewalk with chalk (we always had chalk in our pockets), and we threw safety pins. And I always felt pretty good at hopscotch, one of the few games I felt good at. It's fun to think about it, because it's a bygone era. We always played jump rope. I was not an expert at the really hard jump rope, like double dutch, but I was pretty good at it. My friend Gloria Golden was really good at it. Her mother and my mother were really good friends. She had a little brother named David. Sometimes we played ball against the side of the wall, but that was more a boy's game. We also skated around the block, and I fell many times and constantly had bruises on my knees.

One boy I can think of vaguely that I liked was named Selig. The other boy I liked was Bobby Simon, the son of Mildred and Billy Simon, my mother's friends who lived in Sunnyside in Queens.

I adored Sunnyside. That was my dream—to live in Sunnyside with a house and a yard. That's where we went when my mother and father played tennis. How they learned tennis, I'll never know.

I went to P.S. 173, and it was a short walk, just two blocks from my house and across one street. Before we left school every day, we recited, "Cross at the corner and no place else." Once I was slightly clipped by a car. It didn't hit me, but I felt as if it did, and I fell down. I went home and then back and was late for school. I was marked down, and marks were so important. I wanted to get all A's. One day in Miss Anspacher's class, I spoke to someone else, and that day, I got a B in deportment. I know how terribly it hurt me, because I can still see that B in my mind's eye. I really wanted all A's.

I was taken out of kindergarten after two or three weeks. I remember the feeling of it—the teacher and principal walking up and down the aisles, looking at people's handwriting. I must have spelled my name correctly. So they placed me in first grade. And then I skipped 4B and 7A. Therefore, when I later went to high school, I was the youngest in my class. But that's another story.

I think every child wants to shine for something. And what I liked to do most was write poems and be in plays. And in fourth or fifth grade, we gave a play. This one was something like "The Queen of Hearts," and I didn't have a major part, which of course I didn't like, because I felt I was entitled to it. I was one of three pages who carried the tarts. And I decided that I would do it so well that they would notice me. I had no words, but I was supposed to sneeze. And I really sneezed. I worked up a sneeze, and I produced a real one. And everyone commented about how good that sneeze was. And I was really pleased about that.

Being in plays was a really important part of my life. We gave plays at home. We had a kind of dining room, but it wasn't used for that, because we needed it as a bedroom. But the doorway was a large opening, leading into the hall. So the audience sat in the hall, and we presented our plays in the doorway. It had to have a sense of a stage; that was really important to me.

Through all those years that I lived there, till the age of 11 or 12, a really important part of my life was going to the Heckscher Foundation every Saturday. In the morning, I would paint in oils, and in the afternoon, I would rehearse plays. It was all my mother's doing. She wanted us to have whatever we could have to enrich our lives. There were very few plays written for children; there were just parts in grownup plays. Some were Shakespeare. The woman who ran the art and drama classes was named Fairfax Craven. She had come from a city somewhere in the South. She was very stylish looking, very thin, with red hair. And her mother was always there, sitting in the back.

I did like a boy who was in that class. His first name was Jules. He had dark skin and black hair. He was Romeo, and I was Juliet. He wasn't very good as an actor, but I liked him. The balcony scene was one of our productions. Donald was in all these classes, too. We rode alone on the bus across town, which to me is incomprehensible now. I loved it, I brought my box of oils with me every week; I can still remember the smell. We did some charcoal drawing, too.

Once I decided that I would organize a theater production on 173rd Street. I found out about an empty apartment, and we all went in there and started to rehearse. I think it was a kind of musical, because there were a lot of people. How do you suppose we got in? The apartment was not in our building; it was down the street. As soon as we were discovered, we were told never to do this again. But it was very exciting while it went on. Donald and I both decided we had stardom in our future—if only we could be discovered.

Donald and I, with this enormous wish, did a play every night when we went to bed. We had the same bedroom till I was moved into that so-called dining room when I was 10 or 11. And sharing a bedroom was really very good, because we could make up this play we called the Tom & Jane Hour. I would say, "Oh, Tom!" and he would say, "Yes, Jane?" And we would say together: "It's the Tom & Jane Hour!" And that went on for many, many years. We would make up stories till one of us fell asleep. I can't remember any of the plots, but it was very important to us.

Charles Ruggles and Mary Boland were a comedy team around the time when the N.R.A. (National Recovery Act) was first announced by President Roosevelt, and there was quite a bit of propaganda about it in the newsreels, including routines done by them. When they would come on, Mary would be looking at the newspaper, and she would say, "Nrah? Nrah? What is this, darling?" And he'd say, "That is the N.R.A." and proceed to expound upon all the great things that the N.R.A. would do. And that became the model for our skits at the time. The grownups would sit down, and we would produce it.

Gloria Golden was a friend I had the whole time I lived in Washington Heights. She was thinner and smaller and a tiny bit younger than me. I think I was very bossy with her. Her mother was Rose Golden, my mother's very close friend. I think my mother needed her, because her marriage was difficult, and Mrs. Golden admired my mother greatly for her ambition and for how well she did everything. Gloria's father was Barney Golden, an umbrella maker. He never spoke, but he smiled. They came for dinner sometimes, and we went there, too. It was one night when we went for supper at their house that I came up with the idea for Pirate Joe. I said, "Let's put a note in the little crack between the leg and the seat of this chair." We made a map of a treasure island and put an X with a skull and crossbones where the "treasure" was hidden. We wrote on it "Here lies the treasure of Pirate Joe" and crumpled it up and stuck it in that crack in the chair. And it fit perfectly. Then we got Donald to look at it by telling him, "Sometimes, pirates put notes in trees, and when they make the furniture, the note stays in the wood."

We immediately captured Donald's interest with the map, and from there we had a lot of fun, every day for the next few weeks. I was really excited and left other notes around the house, which he found with my encouragement. He couldn't have been more than six. Then one day, Gloria and I dressed up in costumes, and I pretended to be Pirate Joe, and she was one of the sailors. When Donald came home from school, we told him who we were, and he wouldn't believe us. "You're my sister!" he said.

The next day, I wrote another note that said, "Some people are pretending to be me. Don't believe them." Found a purple tin Louis Sherry candy box, and I put a lot of fake jewelry, some funny old bracelets from the Five & Ten and probably some pennies, and I went to the park and dug a hole and put it in. Then I drew another Pirate Joe treasure map and offered to help Donald follow the map to the hole, which he did with great joy—and he also showed it to my mother. And it was at that point that she called a halt and told me I had to tell him the truth. I told him, "It isn't true. I'm Pirate Joe." And he said he already knew.

Another Donald story, about when we were still sharing a bedroom. I teased him about one of the so-called plays we were giving. I said, "I'm Peter Pan. I'm in Never Neverland." And he said, "No, you're not! You're Barbara, and you're here!" And I said, "No. I'm in Never Neverland." And he became extremely angry, and he picked up a stick, maybe left from a balloon, and he hit me very hard with it, and I began to screech, "Owwwww!" very loud, whereupon my father came in, and he was very, very angry at my brother for having struck his sister with a stick. So Donald was blamed, when it was really my fault for teasing him. He got the short end of the stick that time…

My father wasn't there all the time, but he was there that night. He had a huge influence on us—huge. It mattered to him what books I read. He wanted me to know the plays of Shakespeare. He read me *Julius Caesar* and *Romeo and Juliet* when I was very little, not more than six. And he was extremely angry once when he found me reading a junky magazine, something like *True Romance*. He threw it away, called it a waste of time. He made sure I read Dickens, *Oliver Twist* and *The Old Curiosity Shop* and *David Copperfield*. Later, I had to read Thackeray. So I was very familiar with the idea of good books from an early age. He wanted me to read them, so I did.

Also, I memorized a lot of poems for him and recited them. Donald did, too. The most unusual one that I memorized, and this was definitely a reflection of my father's personality, was "The Ballad of Reading Gaol," a book-length poem by Oscar Wilde. It had a totally depressing theme. And I memorized the whole poem. When I got to Birch Wathen, and somebody asked if we'd like to get up and recite a poem, the teacher was totally nonplussed; she wasn't expecting this stream of words about life in jail for a murderer: "Each man kills the thing he loves, by all let this be heard. Some do it with a bitter look and some without a word. The brave man does it with a kiss, the coward with a sword." I just thought it was very dramatic.

The other influence from my father: We used to take walks with him. He took us across the George Washington Bridge. He called it a hike. Sometimes we went to Palisades Park. All these things were very important to me. He had a very strong personality and was very charismatic and affected us greatly. He was funny, too. He loved to tell us funny things and make us laugh. He was a great storyteller.

I remember walking with him, holding his hand in the park, and he would say he was practicing his summation. I knew he was a lawyer, and I thought he was someone who defended good people against bad people. He loved to quote, "Friends, Romans, and Countrymen, lend me your ears. I come to bury Caesar, not to praise him. The good is oft interred with the bones…" He knew the whole speech, and he gave us such a strong feeling for the importance of words.

Barbara Talks About Mollie's Family

June 2007

All of Mollie's brothers were very short. All of them were quiet and rarely spoke. All of them married gregarious women, and they sat silently.

Sam had the biggest head and was "puffed up" in a way. He was a pharmacist and loved to sing. He lived in Elizabeth, NJ. At gatherings, he would stand up and sing arias. He would have loved to be a singer. His wife was Bella. She was stout, kindly, and had a mellifluous voice and beautiful diction. Their two children were Jules and Sally, a little younger than me and Donald. Jules had problems. How it all worked out, I don't know. They adopted Argentine as their last name.

Marcus was the oldest. He was a dentist. His first wife was Renée. I think it was an arranged marriage. She was taller than he was, had marcelled red curls, buxom, had a European accent, a snooty expression, and was extremely interested in material things, jewelry, who inherited what. They were very possessive of things they thought they inherited. They lived in Schenectady. She would sit like a queen, and he would say nothing. They had a daughter and son, a little older than me and Donald. Arthur was the son; I don't remember the daughter's name. Both Marcus and Renée had red hair, and so did their children.

A few years after Renée died, Mollie gave a party. She had become friends with Florence Herzog, whose daughter, Harriet Herzog, was my college roommate. Florence was a divorcée, a professional woman, an administrator, very bright, sociable, fun to be with. She was the director of the YMHA in Mt. Vernon, NY. She and Mollie were a lot alike. During the party, Florence ran into the kitchen and asked Mollie, "Who is that cute little man?" It was Marcus. They got married, and Marcus smiled all the time. They traveled, were married 15-20 years. She died in her sleep.

Morris was married to Ida, and their daughters were Selma and Pearl. Morris was a gentle, lovely, sweet man with a lovely smile. He looked like Mollie, and they liked each other. Like

Sam, he was a pharmacist. He was also a handyman and carpenter around the house. Unfortunately, he had a lot of difficulty during the Depression. Ida was a nice, short, stout, warm-hearted and gregarious woman with a pretty smile and dark hair. She had had infantile paralysis and had a lame leg.

Her parents were very protective of her and brought food to Ida and Morris after they were married, because they didn't think Ida could learn how to cook. Then came Passover. Ida insisted she would do it herself. She invited the family, and it was wonderful. Selma and Pearl were like Snow White and Rose Red. Rose Red was Selma—serious, good student, helpful, outgoing, friendly, and not self-centered. She went to Brooklyn College and worked as a statistician for the federal government. Pearl was always wearing makeup and talking about boys, always talking and playing with her hair. She flirted with Donald and my father in obvious ways. She had lots of boyfriends. She married Danny, had two children, both boys. They moved, ending up in Florida. Danny died in a car accident. Pearl is still alive and still has lots of boyfriends.

The Brisket Story

October 2008

In our house, we celebrate Hanukkah with brisket. Smells of wine and onions and simmering meat juices stream through our rooms, along with memories—some only fables, partly known. The recipe, I've been told, comes from Abramson's Strictly Kosher Restaurant, at 106 East Broadway in New York City, where, in 1915, Joseph Abramson stood at the register accepting cash and comments. "Good Yontif...The roast, as usual, the best...and the stuffed cabbage, only at Abramsons..."

I see Sarah, his wife—my husband's grandmother—rising in the cold while the children are asleep, descending the stairs to the restaurant kitchen to pierce the meat. It has been roasting slowly, slowly, all night. She tests it for tenderness and spoons its broth to her lips, reviving images—her grandmother, in a Russian village, bent at copper pots, stirring, sipping... proud, austere eyes narrowed in concentration. Sarah never speaks to her children about her grandmother, dead in Russia, or of other Jewish graves, or of hunger or fear in the old country.

She doesn't have time to teach her recipes to her children—not the smart daughter Eva who will win the highest grades in all New York; not Margolia (who will change her name to Augusta), who plays the piano like an angel; not her son, who will die in the influenza epidemic of 1918.

But when Augusta marries her brilliant lawyer husband Ben (he has eaten many meals in Abramson's restaurant) and moves to a brownstone on Bank Street in Greenwich Village, Sarah moves too—to the apartment upstairs. She is thinner now. Joseph has died, and the cancer that will kill her at age 56 has taken root. Now, there is someone to tell the story of brisket to: How to brown the meat to a succulent sheen, to add the right amount of garlic, parsley, salt, and then let the tightly covered pot stew six hours, maybe seven, maybe eight, seeping and seeping into a rich brew.

Anna, the housekeeper, daughter of Negro slaves, who'd come North from the threadbare south, the Depression South, sleeps in the room behind the kitchen. She adores Sarah's small grandson, Walter, and loves to cook, and she learns the mysteries of meals served at Abramson's Restaurant. In honor of Sarah, Augusta's house is strictly Kosher. Anna obeys the Jewish ritual laws, but adds her own—laws devised in southern kitchens, sweet and aromatic. "Sugar brings out flavor," Anna says, adding a pinch. Her brisket is redolent of honey, its hue deep gold.

One summer, Anna goes home to Laurens, South Carolina. Perhaps because she has forgotten the ways of southern towns, forgotten to watch her words, lower her eyes or voice, show what people call respect, meetings are held. White hoods are worn. Frantic, Anna calls New York, and Ben and Augusta telephone a friend who finds her, packs her on a night train to safety. I wish I knew more; it is part of the handed-down fable, and now, details are lost.

But what I can tell is that Anna, in old age, sits on a black wood chair in the kitchen, opening the oven door to peer at the lisping meat, scooping sauce, and pouring it reverently over her brisket, blessing it. She rises on bowed, lisle-encased legs, wide hips sore beneath the blue apron, and retrieves red wine to pour into the pot. She orders Augusta's daughters, now grown women, to set the table, fetch a bowl, toss the salad. I, too, am in that kitchen—married to Walter, making notes on Anna's brisket. I watch her chop and sear and baste, planning my own celebratory meals.

The years turn. Children become mothers. Mothers become grandmothers. One December day a call comes from Florida. My daughter-in-law (daughter-in-love, as someone has said) wants the recipe for making brisket to serve her family, her mother, father, sisters and brother, for Christmas dinner. Excitedly, I spill instructions into the phone—when to add bay leaves, carrots, when to baste, how low to keep the flame. "You'll need a heavy pot." "I have one, yes," she says.

My daughter-in-law is Catholic, devout. For her, and all the members of her family, Christmas day is holy. And on that day, they place upon their tongues the recipe that came across an ocean, wrapped in Sarah's memory, a century ago. That year, the seventh day of Hanukkah falls on December 25th. In both our homes, candles are lit, for miracles.

The brisket's fragrance flows, too, in both our homes. And I think now, as I did that day, this must be the hopeful boundary where peace begins. Here, in a strong vessel, where sap bleeds from a dark muscle cut from bone, where an essence of memory and love rises and glows.

Gus Scheiber's & Lillie Hellerman's Memories of Childhood

Interviewed by Barbara, December 1988

Grandma Gus Scheiber and Lillie Hellerman, lifelong best friends, died within a week of each other in 1993.

Gus

I remember walking up the iron staircase with an iron railing, and a man was coming down. You'll see how foolish I was. He was carrying a bag, and he said, "Would you like a taste?" I said yes. You know what it was? Starch—what you use for clothes. I never tasted anything so bitter.

I was born on Delancey Street. There's a movie now—Crossing Delancey Street. My father came here first. My oldest sister Frances was born in Russia, in Bialystok, and my father never believed she was his child. He was terrible to her, never wanted to have anything to do with her. He could be harsh, but loving, too. He loved children. You know how he showed them? By pinching. Grabbing them. It was too much. My mother was beautiful, very sensitive. She kept her hurts inside.

We had maypoles and dancing in Van Cortlandt Park. I remember they passed out twigs with real blossoms, and I pushed forward, saying, "Me! For me!" A boy gave me a beautiful bunch. I don't know how it happened, because I was such a ninny, I never knew what was going on, I was floating off the ground. I gave this boy my address: Abramson's Strictly Kosher Restaurant on East Broadway, and he came! I was so angry, so naive. I wanted him to leave, and somehow I got that across. His name was Augustus Twig. What do you think of that?

When I graduated from Washington Irving, we had daisy wreaths made from cotton and leaves. I thought they were lovely. At camp, I wore my wreath to dinner, and one camper teased me: "Why are you wearing a fake wreath when we have real daisies right here?" I left the dining room and cried.

We walked across the Williamsburg Bridge. Once, I remember, I was so proud of myself for something I said. I walked across with a boy I liked, and we saw a fire in Brooklyn, in the distance. I said, "It looks impressive from here, but if we were up close and saw all the damage it was doing, it wouldn't seem spectacular at all." I thought, pretty good, Gussie. I guess I had a few thoughts. I was really pleased with myself.

Lillie

My father was a tailor, a master tailor. He had been apprenticed to a tailor when he was a boy. He was in the Czar's army, traveling as a tailor. That's how he met my mother. He was from Latvia, and she lived in Moldavia, nearer to the Middle East. She cooked different dishes—hamantaschen with farfel and ground nuts and honey, and a different kind of dough. He became a journeyman tailor and then a master tailor.

My oldest sister was born in Russia. She was a hellion, terribly spoiled, the first grandchild. She married a doctor. My father was opposed, because he didn't come from a good family. He turned out to be a womanizer.

I was the third. When my mother died, my older sister left high school and took care of the house. There were three of us. We lived in a railroad flat. The front room was the parlor, the back room, the kitchen. The two rooms in between were bedrooms. There had to be a window cut in the kitchen and the parlor so the bedrooms would have light. We had running water and a toilet, but no bathtub. On Fridays, we went to the public bath. The water had to be heated on the stove—coal in the winter, wood in the summer.

My mother used copper pots she brought from Europe. After every Passover, when she made gefilte fish, the tinsmith came to re-tin the inside. We sold all that. We didn't want to take care of it after my mother died.

We had a huge copper pot for laundry. You would soak the laundry overnight and then put the pot in the stove to boil and stir it with a huge ladle. The kitchen was filled with steam.

We started a club in high school to learn about the world. We would meet in each other's houses. Then we decided we would look for a settlement house for our club. We selected a search committee of three girls. We went to them all—Henry Street, Grant Street, Madison House. Madison House was small, you were a person there, so we decided to go there. Augusta Mayerson welcomed us and assigned us a leader. She gave our club a name—you'll never believe it, I'm embarrassed—The Thoughts Worthwhile Club.

The other club we joined—Bobwhite—was different. They went on trips—boys *and* girls! There was a special flower we were looking for—anemone, or May flower. You can't find them in this area anymore. Howard Bradstreet was our leader. He got us all out to look for certain flowers to teach these inner-city Jewish kids about nature, about the world. We would push the old, dried leaves away very carefully and touch the brown leaves, not the green ones, and when we found the flower, we would say a prayer.

He took us to City Island—it was his discovery—and we camped there overnight. All the other trips were day trips. We took the ferry to New Jersey and then the train, and we hiked along the Palisades. We hiked everywhere. Van Cortlandt Park was country—we hiked there. We went for four hours by train to Suffolk County in Long Island. That was where we found the anemones.

On Friday night we had dances.

Gus: You left out—who played the piano for the dances?

Yes, of course, Gus played the piano. Ben and Ike—they were *directors*. They stood in the doorway and watched.

Allen Street was where all the brass and copper was sold. Orchard Street—people come from all over the world for suits there now. My father had a custom tailor store near there. He did very well. We were better off than many other people. He opened a second store uptown. But when the Panic of 1907 came, he had to close that store. My oldest sister was his right hand. She helped him in the store.

I worked after school during high school. Everyone did. I sliced bars of cream cheese. Someone else packaged it. And I worked for my father, doing the office work and other things in his shop. Suits were cut from a fabric that had to be soaked by a sponger, so that it would be pre-shrunk. I washed, then cut the fabric. My father cut patterns out of canvas. He made coats—not pants. Pants were not made by hand, only the button holes and flies.

I also worked at Loft's. The first two days you could eat all the candy you wanted. After that, you couldn't look at a piece of candy.

I wanted to go to Normal School. My father said I should go to commercial high school. I wanted to go to academic. He said, try the commercial, then if you don't like it, you can go to academic. I didn't like commercial, so I had to switch from bookkeeping to algebra and geometry and had to make up all my academic courses to stay in my grade. I did two years in one.

The camp was called the Trolley Car Camp. Cal Sielman had the idea. When they electrified the trolleys, there were all these horse-drawn cars, and no one knew what to do with them. She conceived of the idea of having the cars carried up the river by barges to Orange County. Then they were pulled by horses for miles to the camp site, where they were set up as dormitories. The seats were taken out, and thin cots were put in on either side. At one end of each trolley, there were pitchers and bowls for washing. You got the water from the creek. Gus' mother didn't want her to go to camp, because it was traif. She was only allowed to go if she didn't eat the meat meal. So she brought challah and a salami to camp, and every night she went out of the dining room to a rock where she ate by herself. We were all so envious.

The Scheiber Place in Putnam Valley

By Walt Scheiber, December 2001

This is a brief history of the Scheiber place in Putnam Valley, what it meant to the Scheiber family and to Putnam Valley itself. Israel Ben Scheiber, who purchased the property in Putnam Valley from the Tompkins estate in 1920, was born in Poland on March 24, 1891, and was brought as an infant to the United States. He was to be the oldest of nine children of Louis and Rose Scheiber.

Augusta Abramson, his wife, was the youngest of four children born to Joseph and Sarah Abramson, who came to America from Russia in 1895. Augusta was born on January 1, 1900—the first day of the new century.

The Scheiber and Abramson families shared a common heritage. Both families had fled government persecution and antisemitism in their native countries; both sought new opportunities and freedom in America. Both families arrived in this country in the late nineteenth century and settled on the Lower East Side of Manhattan, where they worked hard to lift themselves out of poverty and raise their children to be good citizens of their adopted land.

Ben and Gus, as Israel Ben Scheiber and his wife were called by everyone who knew them, met shortly before World War I at Madison House, a community center and settlement house on the Lower East Side. The settlement house provided educational and social programs for neighborhood young people, most of whom were children of immigrants.

Ben, who graduated from New York University Law School and became an attorney, had volunteered to counsel the younger Madison House boys. Gus—nine years younger—was a beautiful, gifted pianist who played at many Madison House events and was known and loved by almost everyone at the settlement house. She had a deep love of music throughout her life, and went on to become a concert pianist and teacher, generously sharing her talent with others.

In 1919, Ben and Gus were engaged to be married; their wedding took place on December 31, 1919. That year Ben was appointed chairman of a committee of the Madison House board of trustees whose assignment was to locate and recommend the purchase of a piece of land outside of New York City—to become the site of a summer camp for underprivileged children from the Lower East Side. The committee found exactly what they were looking for in the Town of Putnam Valley, on Peekskill Hollow Road just south of Tompkins Corners. Madison House purchased the land and began to plan and build the camp.

Ben decided to search for a piece of nearby property to serve as a summer home for his family and to enable him to stay in close touch with the new camp. In 1920 he found a tract of 40 acres on Peekskill Hollow Road just north of Tompkins Corners. A wood frame farmhouse on the property had been built in 1888 and was owned by the heirs of John G. Tompkins. The Scheibers purchased the house and land in August, 1920, during the first year of their marriage.

The house was livable, but the interior had never been finished. The second floor was unfinished; there was no attic, and no bathroom. There were no front stairs (the Scheibers climbed on a pile of boxes to get to the front door), no front patios, no back porch and no back yard. Gradually, these were added. The small frame building in the back yard was used to store ice, since there was no refrigeration. Eventually, the structure was renovated, and later was used to store tools and equipment.

As the house grew, so did the Scheiber family. The first child, Walter, was born in 1922; the second, Josephine, in 1925 (she died in 1991); the third and youngest, Sarah, was born in 1929. Their summers were filled with games, picnics, hikes, impromptu plays and fun with family and friends at Tompkins Corners—from school's end to September every year.

Ben began to practice law in Putnam Valley as well as New York City. By 1929 his Putnam Valley law practice had grown large enough to require an office there. Ben asked one of his oldest friends, Isaac (Ike) Hellerman, an architect, to design the stone building on the hill, to use as an office, as well as a stone garage on Peekskill Hollow Road. Earlier, Ike had designed the graceful staircase in the main house. The two new structures, the garage and the office, were built primarily by two Italian stonemasons who offered to do the work in return for Ben's legal services.

Ike Hellerman and his wife Lillie had been close to Ben and Gus for many years. In 1930 Ben hired a neighbor, Jim Post—a farmer who owned the property across Peekskill Hollow Road—to build a cottage for the Hellermans on the hill above the garage. The cottage, designed by Ike, cost $3,000 to construct. The Hellerman family lived in it for eighteen summers, from 1930 to 1948, during which time Lillie, a wonderful gardener, surrounded her house and the Scheibers' place with flowers.

But neither Camp Madison nor the Scheibers were completely welcome in Putnam Valley. There were those who saw them as outsiders from the big city; some were hostile toward immigrants or Jews. One small group—members of a secret national organization, the Ku Klux Klan—was dedicated to making America solely a white Christian country. Its members dramatized their beliefs by staging intimidating demonstrations, dressed in white robes, white hoods, and white masks. They erected large wooden crosses at these demonstrations, setting fire to them so that the fiery symbol of their intolerance could be seen for miles around.

One night the people at Camp Madison saw a cross burning on a hillside not far away. They believed it was directed against them, that they were being told they didn't belong here, that they were outsiders, unwanted.

In the days following the frightening episode, Ben thought hard about what had happened, and about the attitudes that had brought it about. How best to confront this kind of ignorance and hatred? What should be done?

He and Gus decided that this terrible event was a challenge to them and to others who cared about the freedom for which their families had come to America. They would work in whatever ways they could to make Putnam Valley a place where all people could live peacefully and with self-respect and dignity.

At the time, Putnam Valley's school system consisted of five small one-room schoolhouses, each housing grades one through eight taught by a single teacher. The general quality of education was not high. After studying the situation, Ben concluded that one of the most important things the town needed was a new, modern centralized school which could provide a better education for Putnam Valley's children.

In October, 1933, Ben organized the first of 102 meetings held during the following year to convince the citizens of Putnam Valley that they needed a better school system. That first meeting took place in his office in the stone building on the hill. After extensive discussions, in October, 1934, the voters of Putnam Valley cast their ballots in favor of a new central school by a vote of 190-72—even though it meant taxing themselves more to pay for it. Ben was elected the president of the first Putnam Valley Central School Board of Education. He served in that capacity for the next 23 years, until 1957.

The school has flourished, and continues to be a model for others throughout the area. Last April, at the dedication of the new Putnam Valley High School, the school superintendent paid a stirring tribute to Ben Scheiber's leadership. She quoted the words Ben had spoken at the dedication of the first Putnam Valley school, "Into our Putnam Valley School have gone far more precious building materials than brick, lumber and cement: for into it has gone the faith of the people of Putnam Valley in the power of learning as an instrument for developing finer men and women."

In addition to the need for a central school, Ben felt that Putnam Valley needed a stronger, more responsive town government to provide better services and to maintain law and order more effectively. He became increasingly aware of the inefficiency and poor quality of the existing government, then controlled by the Republican Party. In the early 1930s he and a number of other like-minded individuals worked to reorganize the Democratic Party into an effective force. In the mid-1930s the Democrats won control of the town government and took steps to improve and modernize it. Ben was appointed counsel to the Town Board and served in that position until 1948.

Never again, throughout that period and after, did the band of Klansmen make a move against newcomers, and in recent years, there have been no signs that the group still exists. Suspicion and fear were replaced by warm friendships between longtime Putnam Valley residents and newcomers. The efforts to build good government and better schools brought old and new Valley dwellers together with mutual respect.

During all those years, the house and office on Peekskill Hollow Road became a central focus and nerve center for major decisions about the town's future. In the quarter century between 1933 and 1958 hundreds of important meetings were held there, contributing to progress in the community. The efforts made on behalf of the town during that period continue to bear fruit to this day.

But the place was the scene of many events and activities other than those connected to town and school business. After World War II, Ben became a prominent labor arbitrator. He presided at many arbitrations in the stone office building, and frequently entertained his colleagues at social events. Gus Scheiber's graciousness, kindness, and warm hospitality welcomed the many friends who drove up from New York City to join the Scheibers for weekends, picnics and get-togethers. Townspeople and out-of-town visitors came to the Scheiber home for concerts by Gus and other musicians. When their house was winterized, Gus and Ben drove up nearly every weekend throughout the year, finding peace and renewal in the beauty of the place, and enjoying time with their friends and beloved children and grandchildren.

In 1948 their son Walter was married to Barbara Gair, the daughter of another New York City attorney, Harry A. Gair, who also had a summer home on Peekskill Hollow Road, two miles south of Tompkins Corners. Walter and Barbara and their children, Susan, Miriam, David, and Robert, spent their summer vacations in the "Hellerman cottage" from 1948 until 1966. The kitchen was enlarged, a furnace was installed, a porch was screened in, and a dining area with a bay window was added.

In 1951, Sarah married Dr. Charles A. Malone. They and their three children—Stephen, Daniel, and Judith—expanded the family circle that congregated each summer. Ben had built a one-room guest cottage next to the ice house. To house the Malone family, he had that cottage moved up the hill to the orchard overlooking the pond. The cottage was expanded into a two-story, four-bedroom house; eventually a deck and a large family/dining room were added.

In 1986, at the age of 96, Ben died; Gus died seven years later, at the age of 93. The house in Putnam Valley continued to be a haven for them both until their very last years, nourishing and enriching not only their lives, but the lives of their children and grandchildren.

Walt's Recollections

December 2007

My father, Israel Ben Scheiber, was born March 24, 1891 in a small village outside Warsaw, Poland, to Rose Scheiber (née Traub) and her husband, Louis Scheiber. Rose Scheiber was born in Poland in 1867. I don't know when Louis Scheiber was born.

Family legend has it that in the spring of 1891, Rose Scheiber decided to leave Poland for the United States. She is said to have walked out of Poland across the German border with her baby rolled in a rug and carried on her shoulder. They arrived in the United States at Castle Garden, in New York, on July 4, 1891.

Israel Ben Scheiber—called "Ben" by everyone—was the oldest of nine children born to Louis and Rose. The others were Anne, Sam, Sadie, Bess, Helen, Fanny, David and Bernie.

The family lived in the Lower East Side of Manhattan. Later, they moved to Bensonhurst, in Brooklyn.

Ben attended elementary schools in the Lower East Side. He graduated from Stuyvesant High School, in Manhattan, in 1909. He enrolled that year in New York University, graduating in 1913 with a law degree (you could do that in those days). In 1916, he obtained a master's degree in international law from Columbia University. He was a great reader, and said he "read through every public library in New York."

To support himself, he taught immigrant students English and other subjects at the Eron School, at night. After he obtained his law degree he spent several months knocking on the doors of law firms before finding a job as a law clerk. In 1914 he opened his own law office at 51 Chamber Street, an office building near City Hall. He maintained his office there until 1965, when he moved it to 76 Bank Street—his home in Greenwich Village.

In 1912 he ran unsuccessfully for the New York State Assembly as a Socialist and was beaten by Al Smith, who later became Governor of New York. Ben became involved with Madison House—a settlement house on the Lower East Side, then called the Downtown Ethical Culture Society. He was a club leader and, among other activities, took groups of immigrant youngsters on long hikes in Westchester County. Later, he served on the Madison House board of trustees and eventually as chairman of the board. The connection to Madison House and the many friends he and my mother made there lasted throughout his life. He also served on the local Board of Education, and it is said that in that capacity, he handed his future wife, "Gussie" Abramson, her diploma when she graduated from elementary school in 1912. They met again in Madison House, where she often played the piano for the settlement house dances. They were married on December 31, 1919.

My mother, Augusta Abramson, was born on January 1, 1900, to Sarah and Joseph Abramson, in New York City. Her mother and father, Sarah Naufach and Joseph Abramson, had emigrated together from Bialystok, Russia. They opened a restaurant, Abramson's Strictly Kosher Restaurant, at 106 East Broadway, in Manhattan, frequented by Jewish artists and writers. Later, they opened a branch on West 32nd Street. Gus remembered helping at the cash register as a young girl. Many of the recipes prepared by her mother and served at the restaurant, like stuffed cabbage and brisket, later became favorite dishes in our family when I was growing up.

Gus was the youngest of three daughters. A younger brother died in the influenza epidemic of 1918. Gus was musically talented and started to take piano lessons when she was seven. Both her sisters were also talented, in different ways. Fannie, the oldest, was a successful businesswoman who moved to Austria in the 1920s and became an exporter of exquisite petit point embroidery. (Fannie returned to this country after the rise of Hitler.) Eva, the second, was a brilliant student and later a successful executive—a groundbreaker in her career in business and public service.

My mother became a concert pianist and teacher. She studied with Samuel Chotzinoff, who was the music critic of the New York Post and was responsible for bringing Arturo Toscanini to the United States to conduct the New York Philharmonic Orchestra and the NBC Symphony Orchestra. She also studied with Wanda Landowska, the world-renowned pianist and harpsichordist. She spoke with deep pleasure of her lessons with Landowska, and of the words the great pianist said to her one day, after one of her lessons: "You have the gift of God." She remembered walking on air as she went home to her young children.

My mother's repertoire ranged from Bach and Beethoven to George Gershwin and Cole Porter. Her performances included two concerts at Town Hall in New York City, many at the New York Ethical Culture Society, and on the city radio stations, WQXR and WNYC. She also taught at the Manhattan Music School and the Chatham Square Music School. Her devotion to family, friends, and the community often left her with little time to practice, and she became adept at "practicing in my head"—when driving from one place to another. She said that she taught herself to think of the piano as "another child" to whom she had responsibility, so that she could allow herself the time needed to concentrate fully on her music. The sounds of music were always in the house. Often, everyone in the family went about their business, played or read or talked while she practiced difficult passages. She played almost till her death on February 24, 1993, at age 93. She felt that the music she played was a gift to the people listening—and that's how it always felt.

One highlight of those years arose from the fact that in 1930 the New York Philharmonic Orchestra had to lay off a number of its musicians because of the poor economic times. Because my parents knew several of the musicians, they came to my father for help, and he suggested that they consider reconstituting the orchestra without a conductor, more like a cooperative. The result was the creation of the Conductorless Symphony Orchestra, which gave concerts for several years.

My mother and father maintained two homes—76 Bank Street, in Greenwich Village, in New York City, and their house on Peekskill Hollow Road, in Putnam Valley, New York. Our family occupied two floors of the Bank Street house; upstairs apartments were rented to tenants, though for a time my grandmother, Sarah Abramson, and my Aunt Eva lived in apartments upstairs. The large living room was the scene of many gatherings of Gus and Ben's wide circle of friends, including musicians, artists, old Madison House friends.

Every summer the entire family would pack up and move to Putnam Valley; in later years, when the house was heated, my mother and father were able to come for weekends during the fall, winter and spring. The town became the focus of Ben's political and community activities. He made lasting contributions to the town's life—described in another section of these recollections. Concerts took place there, too, in the house and, memorably, in the orchard on the hill. Both Gus and Ben were respected and loved throughout the community.

Essays & Articles

Vassar Calls on Clarion:
The Class of '42 Helps Start the Grassroots Offensive

With Mary Draper & Juliet Fleischl with illustrations by Barbara
Published in *Threshold* intercollegiate magazine, February 1943

This summer we helped set up a War Activities Council in Clarion, Iowa. The council centralizes the town's war activities and gives every citizen a job to do in the common effort.

We are native New Yorkers. No one sent us out to Clarion. No one paid our expenses. We journeyed to Iowa to see how the war goes in the middle west. The people out there showed us that they have the spunk and brains to win the war where they have to fight it—on Main Street.

It all began back in February, 1942, at Vassar College. We were seniors. Since December 7 we had all been "straining at the bit" to "get out and do something." Not just anything. For four years we'd been inside "The growth of pig iron," "Hamlet," "American fiscal policy," "Constitutional Law" and "Greek Tragedy." We thought it all ought to add up to some kind of contribution we could make. The boys were going out to the battle lines. The swing shift was hitting the assembly line. There must be some line of attack for us.

Most of the class of '42 felt the same way. We all wanted war jobs. And that usually spelt Washington. The college bulletin boards overflowed with Civil Service offers—OPA, WPB and all the rest. Desks. Files. Overcrowding. Draft Dodgers. Bureaucracy. Red Tape. We wilted.

One night at Vassar, something we christened "The Plan" was born. We would take roots in a typical American community. We would get jobs (waitress, salesgirl, reporter), settle down, and become a working member of the town. After learning its problems, we would work with the people there to mobilize a democratic over-all organization to direct the "Home Front Offensive." Cooperation instead of conflict and duplication. The people on Main Street taking the bit into their own teeth. Friends, rivals and neighbors meeting together in a town hall to thrash out common problems. And the good democratic habit of pulling together and taking the initiative without waiting to be told.

This vague idea took on the glow of a Holy Grail in our minds. Nobody understood what we were talking about. Our contemporaries laid it on the strain of senior year. Only normal. It would all blow over. Our parents were left dazed and bewildered after intense lectures on "grass roots." Among the faculty, there were those who shook their heads and said it would take four or five years to win acceptance in a small community. Other advisors boosted us with talk like: "You're only young once," and "You can get to know a community the same way you get to know people... it doesn't take five years to make a friend." So we stuck by our guns.

In need of more experienced counsel, we went to Washington during spring vacation. We told our story to government officials, newspaper men, labor leaders. The Office of Civilian Defense wished us luck, but offered no suggestions; the labor leaders thought we should go to Lima,

Ohio, and settle there; the bureaucrats generously handed us countless pamphlets. After about five days, we wound up in the Department of Agriculture. They said we really had something. They thought a midwest town would be most receptive to us. Armed with addresses of field workers, we returned to college, chortling, "The Plan's the Thing."

June 20. We were on the road to Iowa. In the past two months we had grilled through comprehensives, last chapters on theses, stifled the nonplussed questions of our families about "the plan," and switched the tassel from right to left. In odd hours we had become "pen-pals" of several Agricultural Field workers in the Middle West. One short but provocative letter had arrived just recently from William H. Stacey, Agricultural Sociologist for the Extension Service at Ames, Iowa. He said he'd be glad to see us if we ever got out that way. Iowa sounded real honest to God Middle West. So we piled our assets into a blue convertible Ford and crossed the Jersey line.

At Ames we made fast friends with Stacey and Ray Wakely, Head of the Sociology Department at Iowa State. Stacey was an energetic idealist who had worked for years for community councils as the best method of getting a town to plan and use its resources for the good of all. To be at all effective, he told us, councils should be a federation of all established organizations—churches, schools, Rotary, women's clubs. "As I see it," he said, "It's out here in the small towns and villages that a new type of democratic organization can grow up. Here's where planning for better and more equal lives begins. If we plant the seeds during war time, they can carry over for good citizenship and intelligent planning in peace."

Wakely got right to work after he heard our story. He took down a map of Iowa and took us on a mental tour. "Let's see," he said, moving his finger up highway ten, "Clarion's fifty miles from here. It's wide awake, intelligent and alert. Pretty typical of hundreds of other towns. Three thousand citizens. If they throw you out you can move on to Humboldt and then Emmetsburg." He gave us names of several citizens likely to welcome us in Clarion, assured us that we would have no trouble finding "bread and butter" jobs, and saw us off with admonitions to "Be sure and holler loud" if we got into trouble. On Saturday, July 4 the little blue car headed north for Clarion. The sun was blazing. The corn was high. The "Community of Tomorrow" was around the bend.

But before turning the bend to the Promised Land, there were a good many prosaic details we had to tackle. Number one, we had to find a Place To Stay. Would we ever find jobs? Would the townspeople, as our city friends warned us, be aloof and suspicious and keep their doors closed? And what would people think if they knew we smoked? Should we admit we were "city gals?" How would four years at Vassar sound?

Problem number one was solved, temporarily, late in the afternoon when a wary but hospitable woman rented us a bedroom with the warning: "You'd better be good girls. My husband's the Chief of Police." Haunted by our shaky credentials, we hastily closed the door and had a furtive smoke, carefully crushing the cigarette butts into an envelope.

Our first friend was Barbara Jacobson, aged sixteen, whose family was old friends of Bill Stacey's. We accompanied her to Sunday School the next morning and shared a pew with her family in church. Before breakfast, Barbara had spread the tidings of our arrival, and after the service, we were met on the church steps by a bevy of town wives, very curious about the three eastern girls. It all came out... how we'd been to Vassar and lived in New York City all our lives. But they didn't freeze up at the news. They seemed to think it was brave and adventurous of us to come to a new part of the country. Without asking too many questions, they were warm and interested.

Reverend Beebe, Minister of the Congregational Church, really got us started in Clarion. He greeted us at Sunday School that morning. Sunday evening, we told him that we wanted to live in Clarion for a few months, and that our most pressing problem was to find employment. He ran the gamut of possible jobs from tasseling corn at thirty cents an hour to waiting on tables at Moore's Coffee Shop. Then the light came. Clarion had a fine school playground unused during the summer. There were a good many children with nothing in particular to do. Had we had any experience taking care of children? We had. With Mr. Beebe's Sunday School lists as a starter, we determined to ring all the doorbells we could in one week and see what happened.

And we rang plenty of doorbells. We began to find our own way, meet the people, get acquainted. We had a stock speech about the value of group activity for youngsters which we delivered brightly to any housewife who so much as opened her door a crack. Our business arrangements were very simple. Two dollars a week for regular attendance, Monday through Friday, from nine-thirty to five. One dollar for half days.

Walking around the shady streets, we found Clarion to be moderately comfortable and well-to-do. None of the houses were lavish, few were down at the heel. A solid-looking red brick courthouse surrounded by neat green lawn rose up in the center of town. The shopping quarter stretched along for about three blocks on Main Street. There was no industry in town; it was a rural trading center with six churches, a library and a school.

By the end of the week news of the three Vassar girls who were running a day camp had blanketed the town. We had signed up about thirty-five boys and girls between the ages of three and ten. The school playground was ours for the summer. We divided the age groups into Rabbits, Beavers and Tigers, brushed up on "Here we go Loop de Loo," "Run-Sheep-Run," and other favorites, and inaugurated "Camp-at-home-in-Clarion" at nine-thirty, July 13. The little ones, from two to five years old, had a happy diet all summer of bears, tigers, elephants, Indians, paste, crayons, and something called "Rhythms."

By Labor Day, almost every child in Clarion was singing "Frère Jacques," tangible evidence that they had "picked something up" at camp. During our first hectic week of canvassing parents for the Day Camp, we set up headquarters in a small apartment. Equipped with a refrigerator and a stove, we were sure our cooking would soar to great heights. Barbara had brought along two old cooking kits with a miniature frying pan and pot in each. Capacity of frying pan: one egg or lamb chop; of pot: one potato. Our friends helped us out. The lady downstairs lent us a big pot. Someone else brought us a good frying pan. The County Agent's wife told us how to make a roast. The farm security agent took us into his garden one afternoon, gave us his knife, and said: "Here, pick all the vegetables you want."

Almost everyone in our generation was gone from the town. We were pretty much on our own hook for recreation. We tried driving all the way to Des Moines to see a movie several times, but we would come home worn out and guilty about wasted tires. We had a much better time staying in Clarion. We could go swimming, or play bridge with our neighbors, or drop in on the Beebes or the County Agent's family or some other friend and eat popcorn and talk. By the end of July, camp was running smoothly, our blue car bore Iowa plates, and we even felt at ease smoking in our back yard under the apple tree. We felt like old timers, like we belonged.

It was time to get going on the "offensive" we had come to Clarion to launch. With a complete list of every organized group in town as our outline for action, we saw about thirty leaders during July and August. We visited them informally, in their living rooms or gardens or offices. As the "three teachers from the East," we had easy entree. These weeks of "just plain talk" gave us a picture of Clarion's war problems and needs. And as we went around, the plan for organizing the town's war effort became more concrete. Our role, as one woman later put it, was to "put a burr under the saddle."

Our hopes were high when we made our first "war call"—on the County Chairman of Civilian Defense. But our zeal was riding for a fall. We found that he was new at the job. The original chairman was "too busy" and relegated his position to the younger lawyer. His idea of his functions was fuzzy, and he felt hampered by lack of funds. He hadn't gotten around to reading his stack of government literature. When we offered to help out with his local war program, we were told bluntly that there wasn't any.

"Besides, girls," he asked, "What's going to bomb us out here in the middle of the tall corn?"

So we went to see other people. On the corner of Main Street one evening, we buttonholed Pat Crow, owner of the town's oldest clothing store. He told us about the paper drive that fizzled out last year. "As I remember," he said, "The little woman and I got together a stack of old newspapers and put them on the front porch. Everybody was making a big fuss about the paper shortage. Those papers sat there for five weeks and nobody took them away. What the deuce do you suppose was wrong?"

We asked him what the deuce was wrong.

"It was the same old story. There were two clubs in town who were planning to collect old newspapers. A lot of publicity went out and everyone started cleaning out their basements. Then each group sat back and waited for the other one to do the collecting. They both just washed their hands of the whole thing."

"What happened to all that paper?" we wondered.

"I'll tell you what happened to ours. We got so sick and tired of seeing it on the front porch that we dumped it in the back yard. The next night it poured and the whole mess got soaked and we threw it out. It was a great contribution to the war effort."

We'd heard a lot about the Campbells. Mr. Campbell was in the last war and was known as a hard hitting guy would didn't pull his punches. Last year, he got sore when the telephone company tried to raise his rates, circulated a petition among the townspeople and scotched the raise. Both Campbells were very active in town organizations.

"You know," said Mrs. Campbell, "I begin to feel almost like a monster when I have to approach someone for the twentieth time for some kind of contribution to a worthy cause. They must want to duck when they see me coming."

"That sure is one thing I'd like to see started in this town," Mr. Campbell corroborated. "It would make so much more sense to have one coordinated war fund drive instead of the half dozen that keep popping up one after the other."

At one point it looked as if our "long view" Eastern friends had been right, and suspicion of us might ruin the plan. We minced confidently into the office of the most respected man in town one afternoon, fully expecting him to don the white plume and lead his townsfolk to victory. We had heard of his reputation... golden-tongued orator, town father, political manipulator. But we were in for it.

"Just what organization do you represent? Who or what is it that sent you out here?"

We were too stunned to reply. Shifting uneasily in our seats, we were sure that WPA, NYA, TVA and other radical New Deal symbols were splotching our faces. Or maybe he thought we'd come to liberate the kulaks.

As well as we could, we described the history of our pilgrimage in Clarion. We were answered by the ticking of the clock and finally, soft spoken but decisive: "I do not care to identify myself with the movement at all. It seems to me you could have done this just as well back where you come from."

We staggered out of his office. After all this, we would end up tarred and feathered, riding out of town on a rail.

But the plan had already become too strongly rooted in the best interests of Clarion for any amount of opposition to hold it back. Our golden-tongued orator was not the kind of man to start a row. Luckily for us and for the plan, he kept a hands-off policy.

In the middle of August, eight of the citizens we had called on decided to plan a community council still further. Sitting around a half-dark living room one night, they hatched the framework of an organization. These eight individuals sent out a call.

Wednesday night, September 2, will always be an historic date to us. It was the date set by the eight citizens for a "town hall meeting" of fifty-five representative community leaders. Because we had done most of the groundwork for the organization and knew the ins and outs fairly smoothly by now, we had been elected to present the story to the townspeople.

By the time school had opened, we had closed the Day Camp and started a Nursery School. We spent our days helping fretful two-year-olds make their first adjustment to the social world and our nights tossing in nervous anticipation of the Big Moment. Sleep was impossible. Usually we'd give up around two a.m., get up and have a quick cigarette. Like Winken, Blinken and Nod, we planned a three-way panel.

As it turned out, our parts in the Wednesday night meeting were only minor and incidental. We served to present a slate, a basis for talk. But it was Clarion's meeting through and through. It was the spirit of free discussion and cooperative action, of the collective will to "do something," that made it a first-rate meeting. At seven-thirty-five someone closed the courtroom door, and the chairman brought her gavel down on the table. For two and a half hours after we presented the opening panel, the townspeople spoke their minds. They reviewed the history of waste of time and effort, of overlapping, duplication, unused ability, the need for centralization.

The plan of action they adopted was simplicity itself. A Central Committee, representing all groups, would act as a clearinghouse. This, it was agreed, was the best way of avoiding overlapping. A town-wide team of Block Lieutenants could carry all community programs to every last family in Clarion. No organization would lose its own identity… each would simply have the service of the overall council in carrying out campaigns.

Would the Council only coordinate existing activities?

The massive superintendent of schools rose in the back of the courtroom: "You've all been talking in terms of campaigns and drives. Every day on my desk there are new educational materials… pamphlets, suggestions for forums. I'd like to see this organization plan a worthwhile educational program. The more we know about war issues, about inflation, rubber, post-war problems, and aims… the better we're going to be able to fight."

"And I'd like to say something about the farmers living just around the corner from our town," Jay Vendleboe added. "Next year they're going to be seriously short-handed. And we all know how important the food production program is. It seems to me that an organization of this kind could recruit labor from the town to help out on the farms."

The council could initiate new programs... activities which no one organization could manage. It could respond to community needs and ideas. It would have the machinery to put blueprints into action. The meeting wasn't all talk, either. At ten-thirty, a vote was taken. The group unanimously voted to institute the "War Activities Council." A nominating committee brought in a slate of ten citizens to serve on the executive council. The list was unanimously approved.

The meeting clicked. Why? Not just because the townspeople were fired up and sounded off freely. There had been a lot of patient commenting on the ground floor before the meeting ever was called. Instead of merely criticizing and talking, people had a plausible solution presented to them. They were offered a way forward.

On September 2, Clarion's war offensive began. Our job was over. The council was in the hands of ten representative men and women... people who knew their town and took their responsibility seriously. We stayed on for another month, herding our troupe of lusty youngsters, enjoying fried "Westerns" with a new landlady at two and three a.m., and watching the new organization get started. It was a period of "oiling up" for full steam ahead. One hundred fourteen Block Lieutenants were appointed. The council members took stock of their new jobs and laid plans for the winter. We were thoroughly dispensable.

A premature snowstorm in the middle of September was almost a signal to leave. At the end of the month we sold our household equipment for the ignominious sum of $2.50 and made the last rounds of our good friends. The people out there found there was plenty they could do for the war... not because they feared bombing, but because they sincerely wanted to "count" in the national effort.

There are Clarions all over the country, where men and women want to pitch their stakes firmly for victory and a lasting peace. With a strong and purposeful line of offense on every Main Street in the nation, this can truly be a "People's War."

MY DAY
Three Vassar Girls Show Civilians How to Aid War Efforts

By ELEANOR ROOSEVELT

THURSDAY—Yesterday morning I had a press conference, then a few people came to lunch. In the afternoon, the Chinese Ambassador and Madame Wei came to see me for the first time. I asked them as much as I could about the conditions of the children in China. They have not been home for eight months and in that time, of course, where a country has been at war so long, there must be very great changes.

In the evening, Mr. and Mrs. Robert Hawkins, from Nevada, were with us. I invited Dean James Landis and Mr. Philip Bastedo, from the Office of Civilian Defense. Three young Vassar girls also came to dine.

These girls tried a very interesting experiment on leaving college. They made up their minds that all their friends were trying to go to work in Washington, so instead of doing that they picked out a community which they did not know at all, to see if they could do some work to arouse it to its own responsibility in this war.

* * *

THEY went to Clarion, Ia., and established a day school for children during the summer months. The place was not big and so they soon made friends and came to know almost everyone there. They received advice

My Day:
Three Vassar Girls Show Civilians How to Aid War Effort

By Eleanor Roosevelt
October 16, 1942

Yesterday... In the evening, Mr. and Mrs. Robert Hawkins, from Nevada, were with us. I invited Dean James Landis and Mrs. Philip Bastedo, from the Office of Civilian Defense. Three young Vassar girls also came to dine.

These girls tried a very interesting experiment on leaving college. They made up their minds that all their friends were trying to go to work in Washington, so instead of doing that they picked out a community which they did not know at all, to see if they could do some work to arouse it to its own responsibility to this war.

They went to Clarion, Ia. and established a day school for children during the summer months. The place was not big and so they soon made friends and came to know almost everyone there. They received advice from the state college and, after a few weeks, started an overall plan for civilian participation in the war effort.

Now they are back and most anxious to see their pattern tried in other places and to work on it themselves as their contribution to the war effort. It seems to me that they have been enterprising and far-seeing, because in planning to use this organization for the present, they are laying the foundation for post-war activities on an intelligent basis.

What Kind of World Do You Want?

Published in *Seventeen* magazine
February 1945

Aw, why don't you grow up?

That's what your big brother used to say to you all the time, remember? It's funny how long ago that all seems now. It's hard to believe that the soldier whose picture stands on the piano is the same roughneck who used to boss you around. But it is. He has done what he was always commanding you to do—he has grown up.

It came as something of a shock, you remember, when he strode into the house in his uniform for the first time. The tousle-haired kid who once hoarded marbles and bottle-tops seemed to have disappeared completely. The funny thing was, you couldn't put your finger on exactly what was different about him. Then your brother said something that rang a bell. He said, "The army's given me pretty big shoes to wear. It's going to take a lot before I really fit 'em." And he didn't mean size twelve and a half. He was talking about the new responsibility that had suddenly been handed him.

He's overseas now, and the letters he writes home sound as if the shoes are beginning to fit. People used to say, "There's no school like the school of hard knocks." Well, a foxhole is probably a school in itself, and there's a special kind of education a guy seems to get in the turret of a plane or on the deck of a ship. It's not only the military know-how that becomes second nature. It's something much bigger.

He probably steers clear of using words like "democracy" and "human brotherhood." Words like these get slung around too easily, and what he has learned is simpler and deeper than words.

Perhaps he spent the last few seconds before H-hour on some LST {Landing Ship, Tank}, sharing a cigarette with a boy he might never have talked to back home. The boy was from the "other side of the tracks," but it might have been the other side of the world for all your brother ever knew before. Or maybe he piloted a four-engined bomber through clouds of flak, dependent on the other members of the crew for his life, just as they were for him. The crew came from Kansas and Brooklyn and Santa Monica and Wichita; they were Protestant and Catholic and Jewish—but those weren't the things that counted. And those weren't the things that counted if he was slogging through the mud and fog in Italy, or laying for snipers in Tarawa, or manning an anti-aircraft gun aboard ship off the Philippines. What counted was the stuff a man had inside of him; and that, your brother will tell you, doesn't have anything to do with what church he goes to, or where his folks were born.

When he first left home, your brother may have had some petty, narrow-minded prejudices against the very men who are now his comrades. Without knowing why, he may have disliked Jews or Catholics or Protestants or Poles or Chinese. But he's fighting beside them now. He and his comrades are up against the same dangers, eating the same K-rations, sharing the same desire to get home—each one backing up the next guy as if he were his own brother. Just as his buck-private gawkiness wore off in training, your brother's muddled prejudices have worn off in battle.

Maybe he doesn't realize it, but that's just as much of a blow against the enemy as wiping out a machine gun nest or capturing a town. For prejudice is a powerful weapon in the hands of the enemy. It's as much a part of the Axis war machine as the Luftwaffe once was.

Hitler actually believed that he could make us destroy ourselves with our own prejudices. Before the war, he sent specially trained agents to this country for the express purpose of fanning every spark of social snobbery and religious intolerance into blazing flames. Enemy propaganda experts spread all kinds of vicious stories about Jews, Catholics, foreign-born Americans and Negroes.

In speeches, articles and whispering campaigns, they tried to foist this Nazi doctrine of "racial superiority" upon fair-minded Americans. They tried to make us fall for the myth that millions of good, decent citizens—people like our own next-door neighbors—were "inferior" simply because they had different-sounding names, cooked different-tasting food or went to different churches. Our enemies hoped to work up prejudice to such a pitch that we would turn upon each other instead of joining hands against them.

But this didn't work. When the showdown came on December 7, 1941, all the millions of Americans—all of us with our "different" names, "different" racial backgrounds and religious customs—arose together as one fighting team.

Being in the front line of that team is what's made your brother grow up. When you boil it all down, he's found out how to get along with other people, and that's why he seems older. For growing up is really growing out—out of a small, restricted world, into a world where you can live with others.

And what about you? Have you stood still meanwhile, hanging on to all the dislikes you had as a child, insisting on getting your own way, no matter what, paying no attention to the wants of other people?

Of course not. Outgrowing immature attitudes is one of the most difficult parts of growing up. Sometimes new experiences and talks with your friends and older people help. Books help, too. Of course, the quickest way of losing a prejudice is to find out where it's wrong. Mistaken notions about other people often disappear when we test them. That means meeting people, reading history, learning what science has to say. Science will tell you very plainly that no one is born good or bad; that race, nationality and religion have nothing to do with the abilities or virtues of individual people.

Some people know all this and still have stubborn prejudices. That's because so many wrong ideas lie deep in our emotions. To uproot them, we have to find out how they got there in the first place. Once we recognize frankly we have certain prejudices, and we learn how they grew, it's much easier to overcome them.

If you're honest with yourself, you know that you have "pictures in your mind" of many people you have never met. These mental pictures are the basis of prejudice. We aren't born with them. Babies don't have prejudices. Then how in the world do we get them?

It's a long story. It goes back to childhood. We are always amazed at how quickly youngsters catch on to the habits and mannerisms of grownups. In the same way, they also absorb feelings, attitudes and opinions. By the time a child gets to high school, mental pictures are firmly set.

Sometimes prejudices take root in other ways. Very often people make hasty generalizations. Another common cause for prejudice is insecurity. Insecure or unsuccessful people like to blame their failures on others. It makes them feel better, though naturally, it doesn't in the least improve their lot. The same type of thinking often goes on in the minds of people suffering other kinds of disappointments.

Whatever the cause of these bitter and unreasonable attitudes, they have but one effect—to drag us down. A person who carries such distorted notions through life can never grow up. That is the price the prejudiced person must pay. The victims of these feelings pay a greater price. He is made to feel inferior and unwanted. But no matter what the score is between the victims and the holders of prejudice, society is always the biggest loser.

We in the United States have an ideal we're proud of, an ideal we have only partially attained, but toward which we are always moving. That ideal was written into our Declaration of Independence. It says that all people—not only the rich, or the highly cultured, or the aristocratic, but *all* people—have the birthright to "life, liberty and the pursuit of happiness."

That doesn't mean that we're all alike; it means that we have an equal right to prove ourselves: that each of us should be respected and given an opportunity to stand on our own individual merits. That is the basis of what we call Democracy.

This means you, just as much as that brother of yours, who is defending democracy with his life. But before you can help democracy grow out of infancy, you have to grow up yourself.

Outgrowing one's prejudices isn't easy. It's far more difficult than outgrowing the childish habits of behavior that were "cute" when you were seven, but are obnoxious now that you're seventeen. But it's far more important to renovate the way you *think* than the way you talk and act. And it can be done. The key to change is to want to change. If you are sincerely anxious to do something about your prejudices, if you're ready to look them over with the same critical eye you cast on last year's dresses, discarding those that no longer fit, then you've passed the first big hurdle.

The next step is to learn the facts about people whom you don't know, so that instead of having false pictures of racial, religious and nationality groups, you will get acquainted with them as they really are. Let your curiosity be aroused, and plan ways of discovering the causes of prejudice in yourself and your community. You don't have to be in a foxhole to fight for democracy. You can begin right where you are.

Our Town

July 2003

Once upon a time, we lived in a one-room school house with two small bedrooms in the attic, where the children slept, and a smaller bedroom downstairs where they must have stored supplies back when it was a school.

The house was on a dirt road just off West Main Street, with a picket fence and fruit trees an earlier occupant had planted—apple, pear, and plum (once, I baked a plum pie to see if I could, and what it tasted like), and along the house there were quince bushes, and pussy willows, roses climbing at the door.

On one side spread the campus of Grove City High, on the other a park with hills and woods and picnic sheds and a pond where a fountain sprayed the ducks our children fed. Just down the road the Dairy Queen served soft ice cream from an opening in the wall. Our children—two girls and their little brother—could walk there by themselves. The Central School, a mile away, was a castle made of dark brown stone. The girls walked there, too—morning, afternoon, and home for lunch, even in the snow.

My husband, Walt, came home for lunch from his job in the Borough Building, his first real job as a city manager.

The building overlooked a waterfall—Cunningham Falls—named for the town's first settler, Valentine Cunningham, who built a mill. The falls spilled into Wolf Creek; Walt could see it from his window. One winter day a boy slipped from the hill above the falls, through the thin ice, into the stream, and Walt ran from his office with a life preserver, and pulled him out. The story was in the paper—*The Reporter Herald*—the next day.

It was the first time we'd lived out of New York (except for the year before, when Walt went to graduate school in Philadelphia). This was Away, really Away, far from our families and familiar things, not so far in miles (though it did take twelve hours to drive back for Thanksgiving, and we carried sleeping children into the car at 2:00 a.m. so we'd have some driving time in peace), as it was in ways not measured on the map.

The WCTU (Women's Christian Temperance Union) ladies came to Central School, gave sermons on behavior, and at parties, the pineapple juice was spiked with ginger ale and the men would wink—"Watch out—or you'll get drunk"—though rumor said the Humphreys had hooch in bottles in their barn.

The political joke was: Republicans met in the ballroom of the Penn Grove Hotel—and Democrats in the diner. (Probably not even enough of them to fill a booth.)

But church was not a joke. At Central School, before each meeting of the PTA, we were led in hymns and prayers; and a city manager's family did not have the option of private choice to observe or not to observe tradition, and so we drove the children every week to the synagogue in Sharon.

There were four other Jewish families in the town. The rest, for the most part, were Presbyterian, descended from the Scots—which meant that on Memorial Day the glorious parade on Main Street past our house marched to bagpipes blown by splendid kilted sons of Scotland.

It also meant that though our children were invited to visit friends and swim at the country club, we were never asked to come. Yet friendliness surpasses barriers and there were tears the day we left and roots disturbed; a child was born while we were there—Bob, our fourth—and tied us to that place forever. We cut a rose branch, planted it in Maryland, where it flourished at the back door.

As years went by, we thought—it's there. Grove City's there. It hasn't changed. It hasn't. But it has. Forty-five years later the streets still ramble quietly, white frame and brick without pretension, and on West Main the Dairy Queen still reigns—though customers now order inside a glass enclosure, a "solarium," the woman at the counter said, added after Joe Samuels died; she introduced herself—Mabel Laurence, "trained by Mrs. Samuels herself, thirty years ago."

The Howe coffee factory—"Here's Howe"—stands square-shouldered, plain (wasn't it bigger then?), where Pete Beech, prince among men, who married a Howe, whose daughter Connie was in Susie's class, ran the business and the town with joyful confidence: but down the road, our house is gone, even the road erased. And the house that stood behind it where cheery Mrs. Ferguson once skinned squirrels shot by her husband during hunting season, that's gone too; no sign in the green contour that anyone lived on a spot that now flows seamless into park on one side, high school, much expanded, on the other.

A gate's been added to the park, marking the entrance, and benches by the pond, and a deck where children feed the fish. No ducks that day, but still the fountain splashes rainbows; not the same fountain, we were told, just a pump; the old, graceful one taken down to be repaired, and lost, and now the city is looking for the scattered parts, hoping it can be restored.

Across the street the Wigmans' house is there, where Mimi played with "Maurie," their youngest child, gift of their middle age, of whom Mimi, age 4, said disdainfully "she has two-year-old feet;" and beside it, the house where David went to play when he was 3, and waited tearfully for rescue when Ronnie, also 3, attacked and bit him in the shoulder; and the Humphreys', where a mule gave all the children rides in the back yard, round and round a circle as he chewed the grass.

The houses there, the people gone. And Central School—gone. In its place, McDonald's—flags unfurled, snapping in the sun, proclaiming new McSpecials. The story is—the school board put the building up for sale when it decided all the elementary schools should be consolidated, for efficiency; a developer snatched it for a song, then sold it for a handsome profit—like other land along West Main, where fast food and car dealerships replace a neighborhood.

And just beyond the city limits—a Prime Outlet Center—all the bigtime brands, maybe 200 stores, a regional attraction, tastefully constructed, a big success for everyone but the shopkeepers on Broad Street where most of the old stores have closed.

At Burdick's, Tom Burdick, son of the first owner, is shrinking stock into a smaller space, and tells about the plan the Chamber of Commerce has for revitalization of downtown—with lights on trees and sidewalk tables and street events to attract the younger crowd. But the city manager, he says, thinks the plan's a bad investment, money down the drain; the city won't approve.

And yet Grove City is the same, beneath the change. We go to dinner at The Tavern, in New Wilmington, with the city manager and his wife—Terry and Carolyn Farren. They both were born here, raised their children here, after a stint in Oil City, Pa. The population—8,000 souls—is the same, they say; young people tend to stay, now willing to commute to Pittsburgh—an hour and a half away—for jobs. Old people stay, too, loving the gentle rhythm of the town, and senior dwellings have gone up, and nursing homes.

The Tavern is a warp in time—flowered wallpaper, wide-planked floors, the smell of wood, candles on round tables in the small dining room (we went there for birthdays); the menu (not printed, but recited by the waitress) is still the full Monty—soup, appetizers, salad, main course with vegetables and potatoes, home-baked pie and ice cream.

"Something to drink?" the waitress asks, before we order. The choices: lemonade, coke, iced tea. The portions are enormous. This is still Grove Cityland, Western Pennsylvania country.

Beyond the Prime Outlet the countryside rolls with farms. Many are Amish, here for centuries. After dinner, they drive us around. We stop at the new borough building, modern, landscaped (the old building was torn down), with the Grove City library attached (members of the Junior Women's Club collected books for the town's first library when we were there; I remember helping catalogue donations), and an impressive council chamber with paintings on the walls of structures that are lost (like Central School), and needlepoints, meticulously sewn, of the town's history.

They tell us yes, the schools still close first day of hunting season (no bus driver worth his salt would go to work that day), and even though the Cooper Bessemer shut down, the town survived; Prime Outlet helped, brought visitors, new kinds of businesses got started—beauty parlors, Pizza Huts, gift shops, a few antique places.

"It's still our town," the city manager's wife says. "Except now, we lock our doors. We never used to. There never was any crime to speak of in Grove City. Not that there's much now, but you don't feel sure."

The next morning we visit the spot where the Borough Building stood; now you can see the old millstone and the foundations of Cunningham's Mill. We have lunch at the diner—tables and counter set with napkins, coffee cups, and cutlery as if waiting, undisturbed, for our return. We are the only customers, except for one lone man in back in a gray hat.

And then we drive one last time on South Broad Street, for a final look at Chief Burke's house—that tall, wise man from a mountain town—who saw clearly into people's souls but never abused that power. He held our baby in his arms when he heard Bob had a heart condition. "You can't imagine how much you'll love this boy," he said.

He died of cancer twenty years ago, and Carolyn remembers when she was a little girl her dog was lost and Chief Burke went to look for him and brought him home.

Gift of the MRI

Published in *The Washington Post*, March 2007

Her voice is reassuring, but I feel a knot of panic as I slide into the narrow yellowish tunnel. Though I'm old enough to have four great-grandchildren, this is my first MRI. "Don't worry," the young technician says, "It won't take long."

I look up and realize I am totally enclosed; no view of the room, only the smooth, circular sides of a metallic tube. The machine surrounds my entire head and half my body. Beforehand, when I hoisted myself onto the table, the technician put large electronic muffs on my ears and told me she would talk to me during the test. I would be able to talk to her, too. "Keep your arms straight up over your head," she instructed. Then, a mechanical tray rolled me into this strange womb.

Suddenly, there is a crashing sound. It's the MRI machine doing its job. I think of interrogation techniques. Despite the blanket she has covered me with, I am shivering from the cold. With all that banging, if I were at a different angle, suspended vertically instead of lying flat, this could be against the Geneva conventions.

I close my eyes and try humming whatever comes to mind. That blunts the claustrophobia. "I want you to hold your breath for 25 seconds," I hear. Can I do it? As long as I keep my eyes closed, I can. This happens four times.

In between, I sing, softly. I try for no pauses, so I rely on old nursery and summer camp tunes, songs I once sang to my children—all in the key of C and with words I know without thinking—Twinkle Twinkle Little Star... Frère Jacques... Row Row Row Your Boat... Oh My Darling Clementine... childhood melodies to squelch child-like fear of suffocation.

"Please don't sing, it's causing movement." The imaging monster is ultra-sensitive. I conform to its needs. Next, "I'm going to inject you with dye. It's for contrast." I suddenly remember signing a permission form that mentioned the name of a chemical. I have no idea what it is; now it's too late to save myself from poisoning. But I feel nothing, and in a few minutes, I hear "You did very well," and I slide out into safety and freedom.

As I put on my clothes, I am somewhat ashamed of my own ultra-sensitivity. Maybe the machine was a kind of womb—projecting me, with appropriate difficulty and weird sensations, into my Old Age... not just "older," not simply "advanced middle age" or "young old age," but old-old, where I've been, in fact, for quite a few years.

For the next couple of days, I wait to hear that this miraculous camera has revealed suspicious shadows, images, growths. When the doctor calls to say, "Everything's perfect," I am startled into joyous relief. When I celebrate my 85th birthday with my husband and family later this month, I'll really be celebrating, not thinking a good-bye to everyone I love. But still, it's true—I've been born into the brave new world of old-oldness. Born into the last of life. I'd like to make it to my 95th, but, as the lyrics go, "you get no guarantee." A new book, a new moon, an enlightening conversation sufficient unto the day. And, if things get scary, I can always close my eyes and sing.

New Windows

Summer 2007

We had our windows changed last week—a much bigger deal than I expected. A crew appeared at our door at 8 a.m., three young men and their chief, with a truck-full of new double-pane glass and screen panels to fit into 26 spaces of different dimensions. We had been convinced, after 40 years, that our old windows were leaky, inefficient disgraces (most of the screens were warped and torn, and most of the windows never opened) and had to be replaced.

It was the hottest day of the year—over ninety degrees. The young men—thin and agile, with heavy tools slinging from their belts—chipped at worn-out foundations, lifted out ancient panes as if the glass were weightless, then balanced, crouching on narrow sills, to dig and scrape brick and mortar settings for brand new modern installations. A fall from the first floor would at least have broken a leg; from higher up, a whole man. I tried not to look, deciding to clean out kitchen cupboards, since that was the only room that wasn't the scene of flying debris.

None of the young crew members spoke English. I found that out when I asked them if they wanted water, or soda, and ice. Their leader, Dan, was a somewhat stocky man with a sweet smile. He was Korean, and did speak perfect English. I thought the others might be Hispanic, but I wasn't sure what language I was hearing when they shouted to one another. All I was sure of was that these men were sweating heavily in terrible heat, possibly even endangering their lives, in order to improve the climate of our home. In addition, the contractor who sold us the window plan had insisted that it all would be done in one day, and as the sun curved toward the west, it rose perceptibly.

I was refilling glasses of ice when Dan, the leader, approached me. He spoke quietly, but his look was urgent. "May I use your fax machine?" he asked. He had his two hands pressed together. "It's an emergency." I didn't ask what, but he felt he had to explain.

"My wife is applying for citizenship," he said. "She came from China as an exchange student." He had become a citizen eleven years ago, and it had been no problem, but "since 9/11" things were different. His wife's case had been held up again and again with questions and meetings. Various fees had been required, adding up to over $500. Now, she had just received a letter demanding more information. She was distraught, and had called him on his cell phone.

When we finally got the fax running (it had been detached in preparation for the window project), five single-spaced pages rolled out. Dan said the document was full of questions about his wife's role in his window replacement business and that it called for another meeting. It would cost another $150.

He made a call to the office listed on the letter. "I told them we would both be there," he said. "They said no, not both. Just your wife. Alone."

What would be wrong, I wondered, for a husband to come along, to give moral support to his wife? Why was it necessary to intimidate a young woman who wanted to be an American citizen? Why envelop this striving wife and mother (I saw her lovely photo with their two children) in a miasma of suspicion? I thought of my mother, who came to this country from Romania a hundred years ago, at age ten, along with her parents, sisters and brothers—Jewish immigrants who must have wanted, more than anything, freedom from fear. Work, opportunity, yes. But even more—freedom from unbridled power, the fist that could strike any time, out of shadows.

"I am so sorry. I hope it will be all right," was all I said. He put his hands together again, bowed almost imperceptibly. "She is so worried. But we will keep trying." He bent his head toward the men outside, climbing ladders to upstairs windows. "But them...they have no papers. I don't know what will happen."

By nine o'clock at night, the exhausting task was completed. True to their word, the crew—in an amazing cat-in-the-hat operation—swept up all the steel casings, scraps of aluminum and plastic, unidentified detritus that had littered our yard. My husband and I said good-bye, and as I shook Dan's hand, I said again I hoped that everything would go well and his wife would become a citizen soon. My husband gave him an envelope of cash for the members of his team. He gave his smile, then joined the others in the truck.

A few minutes later, the doorbell rang. The entire crew was standing in a circle. "They want to say thank you," Dan said. The men nodded and smiled, and we shook hands all around, saying "Good luck" to each.

"We are the ones who are thankful," we kept saying.

We like the new windows. They open and close easily. Next winter, we expect that the rooms will be less drafty and the gas bills lower. We will hear less noise. We will be better protected, or so we believe, from the storms that gather outside.

Inaugural Vision

January 2009

I woke one morning last January to a miracle framed in my bedroom window. A tangle of dry, coppery leaves clinging to bare branches—leaves that somehow survived the autumn—had arranged themselves into a word. A sudden gust shook the foliage, but when it subsided, the letters were still there, spelling distinctly:

P E **a** c e

Actually, the letters weren't totally distinct. The "c" was backwards. The middle bar of the "E" was missing. But the "a" was perfect—a large, bold lower case "a" that reminded me of the old Remington I used for writing United Press news stories about World War II battlefronts, sixty-seven years ago.

All winter, I listened to newscasts about killings in Iraq, in Afghanistan, in Lebanon, in Somalia, about bombs exploding, melting people in cars. Peace seemed hardly imaginable, even as a word.

That was last year. This is a different January. Bombs continue to explode, images of bodies strewn in streets glare on newspaper pages. But this year, that proclamation of "Peace" outside my window doesn't rebuke me. Once again, it is there—a new configuration of fluttering letters. Again, the "a" is the clearest, but I can still parse the entire word. This year, I read it as a message of hope.

Not so long ago, on a bright October Sunday, I drove from Maryland with my daughter and her family to Virginia, and walked from house to house with my 12-year-old great-granddaughter, knocking on doors, talking to strangers about their candidate for President, leaving literature about Barack Obama on doorknobs when nobody answered. On election night, we gathered with four generations, children armed with red and blue pencils and maps of the United States, cheering as states were colored blue.

I was eleven in 1933, when Franklin Roosevelt was inaugurated President for the first time. I remember the ring of his voice, "...nothing to fear but fear itself." I remember the WPA—"leaning on shovels," critics laughed, but my destitute Uncle Jack got a job he was proud of, lifting one of those shovels. I remember cramming into standing-room-only halls to see Federal Theater Project plays where once-unemployed actors, directors, playwrights, musicians thrilled us with "living newspapers," Shakespeare in modern dress, stories of social justice like "The Cradle Will Rock." My brother was an understudy in one of those plays—"It Can't Happen Here," by Sinclair Lewis—which warned of what could indeed "happen here" if and when an authoritarian president ran roughshod over our constitution. It was a wake-up call to guard our freedom, to be alert to the erosion of democracy.

Today, as I approach my 87th birthday, those days are in my mind. I do not expect peace to reign like magic with the inauguration of Barack Obama. I do not imagine that suddenly the sun will rise on jobs and homes and schools, that wars and poverty, global blight and rampant disease will disappear. But I do believe, and know, that the dire problems we face here and around the world will be dealt with in a new way, with action based on intelligent discussion, respect for differences, understanding of others, and, above all, a firm, uncompromising belief in human rights. I do believe that our new President will bring a remarkable mind, powerful gifts, and faith in the hard work and disciplined moral passion it takes to confront looming nightmares of devastation, waste and loss. I do believe that President Obama will seek the path opened to us nearly 70 years ago by FDR—working as partners with other nations in the pursuit of peace.

At my window, an icy wind blows. Leaves shake loose. The "P" and "c" are gone from the word. But one letter is clear. The "a."

A brittle sun touches the solitary image. "A"—first letter in our alphabet. In Hebrew, the first letter, Aleph, is sacred, to be honored. A light out of chaos. A flag in a cold sky.

A beginning.

Moving

Published in Oasis literary magazine 2014

"Eat your food in small bites," the nurse told my 52-year-old son last May as he lay in a bed in the Intensive Care Unit of Suburban Hospital in Bethesda. He'd been there for four weeks with a breathing tube down his throat and a feeding tube in his stomach. Now, the breathing tube was out and the nurse was telling him how to swallow without choking.

The phone call telling us that Robert was in the hospital ICU came on the same morning my husband and I were waiting for the moving men to bring our belongings to a new home. At 87, we'd both decided it was time to do something practical about our old age, and we'd bought a house in Gaithersburg, a block away from our daughter and her family. The decision brought up our own problems with swallowing as we said good-bye to our home of 46 years in Bethesda—sorting (and discovering) old pictures, letters, clippings, children's drawings, stories and poems that had collected closet dust as we'd rushed on with our daily lives.

While the moving van pulled up the driveway on that rainy April morning, our son was leaving his apartment in Rockville to catch a bus for work. The fog was heavy, and he failed to notice a car coming down Montrose Road. But he can remember what he did see—a spin of color, the reds and blacks of a gas station, as he flew through space. The medics in the emergency vehicle who rescued him did not know if he could survive.

We came to the hospital every day and did our best to calm him as he thrashed his cast-enclosed legs against the bed rails and tried to pull off immense mittens that prevented him from tearing apart the paraphernalia inserted all over his body. The doctors said the blood on his brain made him irrational—he didn't know where he was. Our granddaughter brought an iPod and played his favorite songs; we believed the music soothed him, carried him closer to home.

We ourselves hardly knew where our own home was. On the leafy suburban street we'd left behind, where all our memories still lived? In an unfamiliar house filled with unopened boxes? Here, in the hospital, where, for lunch and dinner, we ate peanut butter sandwiches made hurriedly in the morning? At night, as I tried to stop the ache that came with every breath, I asked myself, "Had I thought that in our ninth decade we would be granted some sort of immunity to anguish?"

Robert is the youngest of our four children. When he was born the doctor told me he had an inoperable heart condition and might not live to adulthood. I cried to myself for a week before I had the courage to tell my husband, and then we both cried. In his first few years, he was so slow to talk and walk, we took our son to a psychologist at NIH for tests, and found out that he had below normal intelligence. By the time he was twelve, he underwent surgery—a miracle of modern medicine—that corrected his heart defect. By the time he was thirty he was doing things the professionals had said would never be possible—reading newspapers, taking the Metro, working as a clerk for the federal government, living in an apartment by himself. Jubilee, an agency that gives help to adults with developmental disabilities, sent a counselor each day to make sure he took his medications and kept his place clean. He bought tickets to concerts. He went to movies. He rode the bus to the Silver Diner with a girl who lives in a group home and asked him to be her boyfriend. That was his old world, one he wishes could reappear like magic.

It is six months since the accident. From the ICU, Robert went to a rehabilitation hospital. His brain healed and he no longer had to stay in a net-enclosed bed to prevent him from trying to climb out—and breaking his legs again. He learned to get up safely, to stand and to walk holding onto an aluminum walker, to slide into the front seat of a car. He is now in yet another place—Summerville—that provides "assisted living." I watch the physical therapist try to teach him to take steps without the walker. She ties a strap around his waist and holds on. He stumbles, lurches, unable to get balance on the leg that had been shattered. Each day, when we see him, he asks—in different ways—often with anger—when will I live by myself again? When can I cook my own meals? When can I earn a paycheck? When can I be independent?

I don't know the answers. We talk about how far he's come. We take him to picnics with his old friends and he grieves for the difference between them and him. I can't pretend to him we know the future; he catches any false note of Pollyanna-talk, exaggeration, or untruth. But I can say this: We'll wake up each day and see what happens. We'll use our brains and our love to help you find new ways to be what you want to be.

And we—my husband and I—will look for new ways, too—quick moments outside the world of pain, times to nurture ourselves. We have been living further and further away from ordinary life, hardly able to talk with friends on the phone—as if they were speaking an alien language. We need to learn to live in this house we've moved to.

In our front yard, the leaves of the weeping cherry tree are gold, the holly berries red. I suck the colors into my lungs, try to see what lies ahead, and remember the words of the nurse when she taught my son how to eat.

We'll take it in small bites.

Speech to the National Association of Regional Councils

Introducing the Walter A. Scheiber Leadership Award
May 27, 2015

Thank you so much (to who introduces me) for your kind and gracious words. And congratulations to Tom Wilkinson for winning the Walter A. Scheiber Leadership award for the wonderful work you are doing as Executive Director of the Brazos Valley Council of Governments. It's a thrill for me to meet all of you and to learn about the exciting regional programs you are building. I know your work calls for round-the-clock dedication, and I know that Walt would be proud and honored to hear of your efforts and accomplishments in striving to reach the goals he believed in deeply. It is very moving to me to have this chance to meet and talk with you about the work that was so close to his heart.

Walt was described as "a superb diplomat." He knew how to bring people together to get things done. But it was more than diplomacy that lay at the center of his leadership… It was, I think, his understanding and appreciation for the differences between us all—differences of background, upbringing, point of view—and at the same time, our commonality—our shared belief in ethical values, values that guided him all his life.

His values had deep roots. His grandparents fled tyranny in Europe in the 19th century to come to this country. He lived much of his early years in a small rural town—Putnam Valley, New York—where, as a young man, he drove with his father to town meetings to fight for the creation of a central school, in place of scattered, poorly attended one-room schoolhouses, and for other community causes.

During World War ll, he served in the Army Air Force as a gunner and radio operator—flying 30 missions over enemy territory. He kept a diary of his missions, and described crawling out onto the bomb bay to make sure the bombs had actually been dropped—sometimes writing very uncomplimentary messages on the bombs themselves—basically, unprintable advice to Adolf Hitler.

Walt often advised young people not to be afraid to change their careers, if they've discovered new work they love. When we were married, he started his post-war career as a lawyer, but discovered that his true calling was work in the field of local government. We packed up our young family; he left his law office to become a city manager—and we never looked back.

After years that we treasured in Grove City, Pennsylvania, and Rockville, Maryland, Walt made another change. He became the executive director of the Washington Council of Governments—and entered the challenging, complex and rewarding world of regional intergovernmental action—the world you all now contribute to so richly.

It's a world that has changed enormously since Walt's day—with many new, difficult and important problems to deal with. When he entered the profession, in 1966, there were about 50 regional councils in the country—now there are more than 500. I remember so well the conference at which this organization—the National Association of Regional Councils—came together, almost 50 years ago—on a sunny day in April. I remember how proud Walt was that day—working hard with the Washington COG staff to make it a success. The keynote speaker was Senator Edmund Muskie—who galvanized the growth of regional councils with legislation setting up federal support for cooperative efforts to solve a vast range of problems. Walt became the first president of NARC—for the rest of his life, a badge of honor.

I know how proud he would feel now—to know the strength of your commitment and dedication to the cause of regional cooperation—and would salute your leadership in building programs responsive to vital community needs. Muskie's vision of federal support came to an end, and now there is far more need for private-public partnership. Time brings change, but the constant through the history of regional councils is the ideal of cooperation—the pooling of effort, despite conflict and difficulty—for the greater good. On Walt's behalf, I thank you with all my heart for all you are doing, congratulate you on your achievements, and wish you great satisfaction in knowing you are contributing to a better society.

In his last years, Walt wore an Army Air Force emblem on his jacket. People often stopped to say to him, "Thank you for your service."

I say, with gratitude to all of you—

Thank you, for your service.

Jewish Holiday Stories

In their drive to create a modern life for themselves and their children, Barbara's parents abandoned the practices of Europe's Jewish ghettos and shtetls—and that included commemorating religious holidays. But when Barbara became a radio producer for the Jewish Theological Seminary's program The Eternal Light in the late 1940's, she immersed herself in learning about Jewish history and heritage. After she and Walt had their own children, Barbara created Rosh Hashanah, Hanukkah and Passover stories that expanded the traditional narratives to highlight the moral and ethical messages that gave them universal meaning—in words the children could understand. Every year in the decades that followed, our family gathered around Barbara and Walt's table to read these stories aloud together—our family tradition, a gift to us from Baba. L'chaim!

Rosh Hashanah and Yom Kippur

Tonight we are gathered together to celebrate the Jewish New Year. There are two special days of the Jewish New Year—Rosh Hashanah and Yom Kippur. Rosh Hashanah means Head of the Year—the most important day.

But head means something else. It means thought, how we think. It means thinking about ourselves and how we want to act, what we want to do to make others happy, how we can show our love and consideration for other people in our families and in the world.

We all make mistakes; nobody is perfect. At Yom Kippur, we think about things we are sorry to have done, things we want to change about ourselves. We apologize for mistakes we've made and decide to do better in the future. We resolve to try our best to be fair, to help others who need our help, to comfort people who are afraid, to behave in ways that show we believe—not in hatred and anger—but in justice and in freedom for everyone.

All of us want to build a world where people respect one another, where everyone lives at peace. Each of us can ask ourselves: How can I do this in my own life, in my own family, in my own circle of friends? The days of Rosh Hashanah and

Yom Kippur are special times to think about how each of us, in his or her own way, can help to create a peaceful world.

The Jewish people have, over the centuries, endured many hardships. They have a saying that means: "You go on. You go on with your journey." When something bad happens, you go on. You go to work and to school. You sing and paint pictures. You play games and laugh. You remember the people you love who have died, and you light a candle to show your love. And you try to do whatever you can to be a good person. The Jewish religion teaches us to show what we believe by what we do, not just by what we say. Each of us, in our own way, can show that we believe in goodness, fairness, and peace.

We say thanks for our beautiful family, for all of you. We love you with all our hearts. As a symbol of our hopes for the new year, we will light the candles on the table. As a symbol of our love and hope for goodness in our lives and in the world, we will dip bread and apples into honey.

Happy New Year. L'shana tova.

The Story of Hanukkah

Illustrated by Barbara Scheiber & Ethan Seidel (age 9)

Today is Hanukkah. Do you know what we do on Hanukkah? We light candles...We eat potato pancakes...and we tell a special story. This is the story:

A long long time ago—twenty-four hundred years ago—the Jews lived in ancient Greece. A king named Antiochus came to power, a king who forced everyone to obey his laws. He declared that the Jews must bow down to a big statue of Zeus. He ordered them to leave their beautiful Jewish temple—the most beautiful building in the world. The Jews loved their temple, and many of them were afraid of Antiochus. They didn't want to obey Antiochus, but they didn't know what to do.

Here is a picture of Antiochus, the king, commanding the Jews to bow down to his statue of Zeus.

One very brave, good man—the leader of the Jews—said NO. His name was Mattathias. He would not bow down to Zeus. He would not leave the beautiful temple. In a deep, strong voice, he thundered: "Whoever is for God, follow me." And he, his sons, and other Jews decided to fight against Antiochus.

Here is a picture of Mattathias:

Mattathias and Judah and his other sons and followers were called the Maccabees. They fought hard against Antiochus. Antiochus had an enormous army, but the Maccabees were very brave.

They fought with sticks against the swords that Antiochus' army used. Antiochus and his soldiers even had huge elephants... but the Maccabees weren't afraid. They fought so hard that they finally won. Here's a picture of the Maccabees fighting with sticks against soldiers with swords and elephants:

When the Maccabees won the war, they went home to celebrate—but they found their beautiful temple broken. Everything was destroyed. And saddest of all, there was only a drop of oil left to light their precious lamp—their menorah.

The lights in the menorah were supposed to burn forever. But how could they possibly keep the lights burning with only one tiny drop of oil? That was hardly enough to last for just one day.

But they poured the oil into the lamp and lit it—and do you know what happened? The oil burned not for just one day, not just two days, but for eight whole days. The light was beautiful and bright—as bright as the spirit of the Maccabees, who refused to give up until they won their freedom.

As the light burned, the Jewish people dedicated themselves to rebuilding their temple as a place to celebrate freedom. That's what Hanukkah means—dedication. That's a big word that means putting all your heart and soul into working for what you believe is right. It means finding ways to help bring peace and fairness, hope and freedom to the world.

So every year we light candles on Hanukkah. We light them for eight days, to remember the miracle of the drop of oil that burned for eight whole days after the temple was destroyed. And we remember the miracle that is inside of each of us—to try to do what is right and good, and to stand up for what we believe is right, no matter how hard it may be. That is our own light.

And now, we will light the candles and say to each other, "Happy Hanukkah."

Happy Hanukkah!

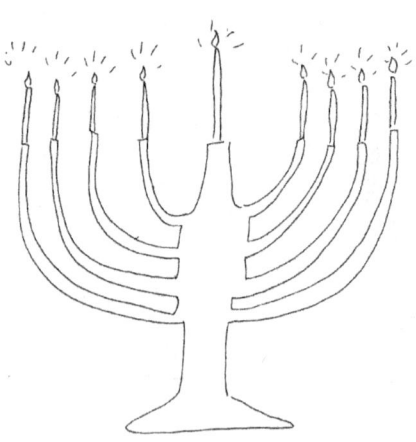

Passover

Illustrated by Barbara Scheiber & Ethan Seidel (age 9)

In the midst of this beautiful season of dogwood and redbud, tulips, azaleas, lilac, and apple blossoms, we celebrate Passover... a beautiful holiday, celebrated by coming together with love and joy. The holiday has, for thousands of years, been marked by this kind of coming together of loved ones—a party of remembrance and affirmation, called a Seder. There are ancient rituals to the Seder, and ancient truths to recite. A Seder is a lesson for children, a time to tell the ancient story. So what would be more fitting than to say our own Seder service in words for the children here today? Let's begin by making sure that the children are comfortable, sitting on a lap or a chair, whatever they like.

The story of Passover begins in a special way. It begins with four questions. We'll listen while the children ask the questions.

Why is this night different from all other nights? On all other nights, we eat bread. Why do we eat matzoh on Passover?

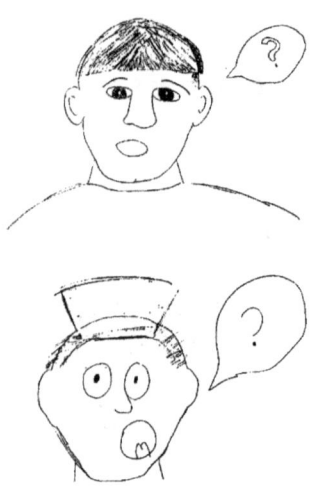

On all other nights, we eat vegetables and herbs. Why do we eat bitter herbs at Seder?

On all other nights, we don't dip foods into each other. At the Seder, we did parsley in salt water and dip bitter herbs in charoset. Why do we dip foods twice tonight?

On all other nights, we sit up straight. Why do we recline tonight?

The Passover story gives the answers to these questions.

Long, long ago, many thousands of years ago, the Jews were slaves in Egypt. The king—called Pharoah—forced them to carry heavy stones to build his palaces. They worked till they fell from exhaustion.

slaves in Egypt

One Jewish mother wanted to save her baby boy from this terrible life. She hid him in a basket near the river bank. Pharoah's daughter found the baby and brought him to the palace to take care of him.

Pharoah's daughter finding Moses

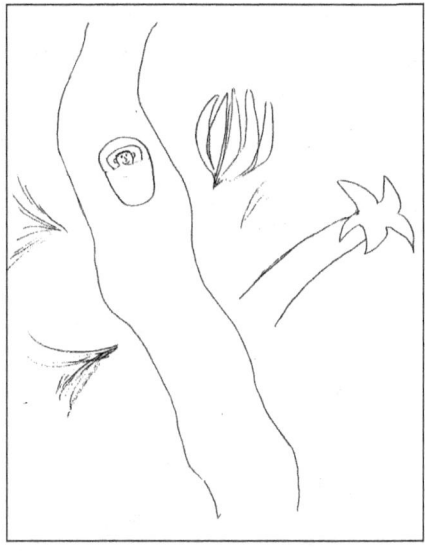

Miriam, his sister, who had been hiding nearby, came, too, to be sure he would be safe. The baby was named Moses, which means "brought out of the water."

Moses grew up to be a kind, good man. He was angry at the cruel way the Jews were treated. One day, he hit an Egyptian who was beating a Jew. After that, he left Egypt and became a shepherd.

While he was caring for his sheep one day, Moses heard God speaking to him from a burning bush. God told Moses to return to Egypt and to lead the Jews out of slavery.

"Let my people go!"

"Let my people go!" Those were the words that Moses spoke to Pharoah when he returned to Egypt. But Pharoah wouldn't listen.

So God sent many terrible plagues to punish Pharoah.

He sent flies that destroyed the crops. He sent a violent storm and icy hail. And frogs—frogs everywhere. Can you imagine? Frogs on your head and knees and toes, all over the bed and table and floor! After that, God sent a darkness that covered the sun.

For each of the plagues, we let a drop of water fall—like a tear—to show our sadness for the Egyptian people, who also suffered for the cruelty of the Pharoah. (Dip finger in water glass, drip once on napkin.)

Every time there was a plague, Pharoah promised to set the Jews free. And each time he broke his word. Finally, God sent the angel of death to kill the oldest son of every Egyptian. But the angel passed over the Jewish homes and saved all their lives.

Then Pharoah finally said yes, he would let Moses lead his people out of Egypt.

The Jews had to hurry to get ready to leave. They had no time to bake bread, so they carried raw dough on their backs—and the sun baked it into hard crackers called matzoh. And that's why we eat matzoh on Passover.

God led Moses and the Jews by day and night—going before them as a pillar of light. At the Red Sea, God parted the water when Moses held up his walking stick, so the Jews could walk across the sea on dry land. When they reached the other side, the sea filled up again, just in time to stop the Egyptian soldiers whom Pharoah had sent to capture the escaping Jews.

Out of Egypt

And so tonight, we can answer those questions. Why is this night different? Because tonight we celebrate our freedom and wish for freedom for people everywhere. Why do we eat bitter herbs? Because the bitter taste reminds us of the hard life the Jews led as slaves. Slavery has a bitter taste, and freedom has a sweet, good taste—so we eat both bitter and sweet things tonight.

On the table are special Seder plates with different foods that remind us of the Passover story.

Parsley—to dip into salt water to remind us of the tears of people who are treated cruelly anywhere in the world.

Charoset—made of apples and honey to celebrate the sweetness of loving one another and being together, safely and happily.

An egg—to rejoice in the new life of spring, now that winter is over.

A bone—to remind us of the pain endured by slaves.

Matzoh—the bread the people ate as they followed Moses out of Egypt.

And we sit comfortably tonight to show our happiness in our own good fortune, to live in a country where we are free to think and act in ways that we believe in our own hearts are right and good. We give thanks for our wonderful family and peace in our lives.

Happy Passover!

Poems

Beginning

I dream a poem
and in the dream
it is chosen
to be read
in a workshop.
"Second place," the workshop leader says.
First place goes to a designer of
intricate silver jewelry—
mine is only words.
But when I begin to read,
there aren't even words
only smudges
on a piece of paper.

Awake, I search frantically,
grasping
for the words
that fled,
grateful to ensnare
these few
on this page.
No prize here.
Not even second place.
Only joy and fear
as I begin to dream
a poem.

To Write a Poem

Cut flesh away—
cut the soft shell that yields
to the clock's turn,
to light and dark,
heat
and cold.

Cut to my spine—
the hidden
chain,
each link a secret
trembling with memories,
sounds, sights,
dreams awakened by
a sound, a voice,
a scent.

Cut to my bones—
tough sponges—
knowing every blink of fear
or lust,
pain or passion
beneath my skin.
Cut to where
truth resides—
waiting for words—
for birth.

Departure

I grow breasts early
at barely ten
(uncommon in those hushed times)
I hunch my shoulders to conceal
my shy new parts,
write poems and
dance my head off
in a modern dance class.
That is the year my father leaves
for good.

In those hushed times
he never leaves.
It is a secret.
We hunch together to conceal
the missing part
of family.

He comes on Sundays
with bagels, lox, black olives.
I read my poems to him.
He takes us to movies
and then
he leaves again.

My poems are not enough
to make him stay.
I dance harder
turning, shaking, spinning
waves
of anger, grief
inchoate desire
dark, moist dreams
concealed.

I dance
for him one Sunday
whirl and leap
in our small living room
until I see him look away
gone forever—
my poems
my dance
mine alone.

Eighth Grade

In eighth grade
I entered private school—
Birch Wathen—
and learned there were two kinds of Jews,
German and Russian.

My Uncle Harry (not a real uncle;
my father's oldest friend),
an elegant lawyer for RKO,
listened to the names of girls in my class—
Heidelberger, Heilbrun, Vorhaus, Gottlieb—
and said
"German Jews."
"Rich," he told me. "Ritzy."
"Your father and I," he said,
"Grew up on the Lower East Side.
We all slept in one room without heat,
the Catholic kids yelled 'Christ killers' at us
and threw stones."

German Jews came a half-century before,
and lived on Park Avenue;
they even had a governor—
Herbert H. Lehman.
In my eighth grade class
one girl took riding lessons,
another spoke French,
had a governess and a doorman.
My uncle fingered the watch
dangling across his vest.
"Work hard. Be a star," he said.
I began to cry.

Until that year,
I played pirates in a park across the street,
gathered moss for a diorama,
ran like the wind from

kidnappers who tried to touch me.
I never knew I had something to fear from
Other Jews.

Divisions

The summer I was sixteen
I traveled to France
with my mother and a friend from school
(the trip was tribute I believe
exacted by my mother
for my father's frequent trips abroad
with another woman).

On the train from Paris
we flirted with the conductor
who stopped to smile appreciatively
at the two American girls.
"Will there be war?" I asked.
He rolled his eyes.
It was 1938.

In Juan Les Pins,
an older man poured champagne
and told me that my name meant stranger.
Not only the first name—Barbara—
(from the Latin)
or the last derived from Ger in Hebrew
but Ruth, my middle name—
"A stranger in a strange land."

In the fall, still sixteen,
I entered Vassar
and did not say Gair,
spelled the Scottish,
and not the Hebrew way,
was Jewish,
or say my father
had left.

Later that year
I learned another girl—
from Memphis—

her accents incomprehensible
to northeastern ears—
frightened of mockery
shut herself in her room
and became
mute.

String
(to my mother-in-law)

I see you on the train
your head encircled in
black braids,
a mass of tangled string
in your hands—
hands so supple they can
span an octave
and break an apple
in two.

It is 1919 and
you are nineteen—
a child of the century.
It will take twelve hours
for the train to reach
Chicago.
You have never been away
from New York
except for the camp
for children of immigrant Jews
and never before
alone.

How little I know
only that you are unwinding
the coiled knots
in your hands
only that
a dancer is waiting
in Chicago
his name is Adolph Bolm
and he has asked you to
accompany his troupe
to play the piano
for his ballet.

Frayed bits have come
through time
this story and that
you said the string
calmed you
as the train sped
into night
leaving behind
the man you are engaged to
marry—ten years older—
already a member of
the New York City
Board of Education.

The family story is
he awarded your diploma
when you graduated
from eighth grade.
Is it true?

I see you quiet, erect
listening to the music
in your head
gypsy sounds whirling
stamping—
black hair unbraided
to your waist—
while fingers discipline
the string.

No tales have come
about the fervor
of those months
(how many? two? three? more?)
the harmony and poise—
motion geometry light song—
delicate, fierce order
intricately strung
into your brain.

Only this:
when you come back
they gather in the kitchen
mother, father, sisters
with their surprise—
a gift for the
beloved daughter
favorite child
bride-to-be—
and hold their breaths
as you unwrap
the prize
to launch your life—

A set of pots and pans!
you tell me laughing
forty years later
seated at your piano,
a slender grandchild
between your knees
small hands resting
on yours.
Play! the child commands
and your fingers leap glide
lament and sing
until the girl
slides away
banging the screen door.
You turn to me.

"Pots and pans," you repeat...
"Life is complicated."
We are in your country house
in gentle hills
a home where celebrated works
are done
by you and your Board-of-Education
husband—like you, a child
of immigrants
whose mother smuggled him

in infancy
across the Polish border
in a rug
to save him from
the specter of harm
to Jewish boys.
He is a slight man
With a will of steel.

The train ride is
a stone in time
hardly rippling the current
of your life.
I only know that years of
tangled string collect in
drawers
and know
how many times you drive away
from these soft hills
to rent a room
in a farmhouse
and sit alone
in silence
decoding Beethoven's
wild math
listening to its secret
order
and turning turning
turning
string from the kitchen
until each knot is smoothed
and once again
the skein is wound
into a single
ball—solid, tight, and
strong.

Piano

The piano is her fourth child, she says,
a concept that assuages
guilt,
forgiving neglect, permitting
hours of devotion—
not gentle doting—
stern service
under the baton
of measure, time, key—
cold, unremitting grammar.
I hear her drilling, drilling
with exquisite instruments—
fingers, arms, nerve paths.
And then syntax explodes,
flows, soars,
releases thunderous gold.
My heart sings
to the burning of stars—
love, joy, pain, ecstasy.
Death.
Birth.

My Mother's Song to Her Children and Grandchildren

I will give you everything
A long green dress to catch the wind,
A crimson coat,
A chestnut horse with satin flanks
As swift as any mounted by
Romanian kings.

And you will know the sun and moon
And all the flowers of the earth
And valleys filled with daisies
That you reap like stars.

And I will silence owls
And lions in their lair
And hold the teeth of darkness
from your eyes.

And in the starlight you will dance
And fly and sing
And I'll embroider roses
While you sleep.

View From My Kitchen Window

Bare branches rise
on rooftops—
decorative antlers—
as if they have no
history
no roots tendrils accidents
deformity or blight.

Even the sentinels
of oak
on suburban lawns
spring full blown
from shaven grass—
poster trees
without a past
or moist dark birth
or secret.

Icicles Hanging From Our Roof

Euclid's beauty—
bare—
slicing
blue frozen light,
daring my eye
to blindfold memory,
tangle threads of past and future,
banish compromise and caution
to the lure of
Euclid's
silver daggers
hanging from our roof—
choosing perfection
over life.

January Robins

I'm not a bird watcher
but I know a robin
when I see one
and today not one
but twenty-one or more
ripple over snowy lawns
while crows and I
in January black
stand watching—
wings folded.

We confer.
Don't they know what month this is?
Are cosmic wires
to the winds and stars
severed?

Will planets rock off orbit
moons turn red
orchids grow
on winter streets
and termites—morphed by heat—
begin to feast
on steel?

To Hang an Earring

To hang an earring
you need a compass
with lilliputian points,
a sharp shift blade
inflicting accurate pain,
and tolerance for blood.
Healing matters less
than inserting
the gem—
a gleam that conceals
the scar.

Twenty Years

So many skies have turned
And whitened trees
So many stars have curved
And realigned
So many words have swung
Against the days
In twenty years.

And here's my hand, not asking
To define the skies and stars and days,
But to celebrate them—
In all their changing
Patterns
And their gifts
Of love and pain.

Again, here is my hand.
Aware, at the touch,
Of the spring-new-green quickening,
Of a young day's singing promise
And the joy of walking in its lights
And shadows
Together.

Here is my hand,
Again.

Light

I never noticed
till the room was dark
that firelight pulses on the ceiling
like a siren
in the night.
Broad sheets of gold,
though the flame is only
a finger,
a dying coal.
Love.

When he is 86
Hershel my stepfather cuts out ads
for achieving
an erection worthy of the name
then hides the pills
so she—my mother—
will not think he has
another woman.

My mother falls
and thinks the medics in the ambulance
are her children
though she forgets their names.
In the hospital they strap her to the bed
after she attacks the IV pole
thinking it is the Czar's soldier
come to steal her brother.

That night, she claws apart the strap
undoes her gown
runs naked
down the escalator stairs.
They stop her in the lobby
and she wails
"Where are they hiding Hershel
where are they hiding
my darling Hershele?"

In Moonlight
(June 2001, for Kevin, Melanie & Jeremy)

In moonlight when
the wind is high
think of Daddy
do not cry
think of Daddy
do not cry.

Dry the tears
of that sad day
when they laid him
in the clay,
clouds came over
wild and gray.

In the darkness
of the night
see him with
your inner sight,
hear him say, "You'll
be all right."

Hear his words
inside your head
"Proud of you,"
he always said.
"Time to lie still
in your bed."

On your back
his hand is strong
just like when
the days were long,
birds were singing
summer's song.

Apple trees
were all aglow,
you climbed as high as
you could go,
touched a cloud.
He smiled, below.

His love for you
will never die,
like stars that swirl
across the sky
like moonlight when
the wind is high.

Think of Daddy
do not cry
think of Daddy
do not cry.

The Stone

The stone fit in the palm of his hand.
It was the white one, with dark brown lines running across,
like the lines in the palm of his hand.
He'd found it in the creek at the end of the street
where he was not allowed to go,
but where he had gone
anyway.

He stood by his mother's bed.
In the light sifting through the blinds,
he could see her sleeping face,
hair spilled on the pillow.
Her sheet was crumpled, the comforter on the floor.
The place where his father used to lie
was flat,
the blanket folded.

He watched his mother's mouth to see if it moved.
If she was having a dream, she might smile.
If his eyes never left her face,
he could keep her from starting to die.

His mother wasn't dying.
But his father hadn't been dying,
and then he was.
One day his mother told him
his father wasn't going to get better
and a few days later
they carried him out to a car
in a black bag.
He was watching from the back of the house,
and nobody saw him.

He rubbed the stone with his other hand.
It was damp.
He didn't want it to be damp.
He dried it with the cloth of his pajamas
and quickly slipped it under her pillow

and ran from the room
so she wouldn't see him
putting it there.

On his way out
he stubbed his toe
and he felt it throbbing when he lay on his bed.
But it didn't matter
because now he knew the stone
would protect his mother
and he was safe.

March of the Signs
Washington, DC, Saturday, October 26, 2002

It rained the day before
And the day before that
So the grass is damp in Constitution Gardens
But the sky is bright
And signs with magic-marker slogans
bloom along the duck pond,
The winding walks and streets,
The watchful marble colonnades.

We come by Metro—Susie, I, and Lili—
Lili, who long ago saw other signs
when at the age of twelve she and her family
escaped by train from Paris, pretending to be German.
George shows up
in the melee of feet and arms and magenta hair
and blue and silver lines of helmeted police,
and we join the
march of signs.

And as the crowd thickens,
expands, grows like a loose-jointed centipede
with not one hundred
but one hundred thousand pairs of feet,
the signs—bawdy, sassy, irreverent,
passionate, angry, biblical,
and peaceful,
move, bob, sway, speak,
testify.

Remember Wellstone. No War.
Oil Kills.
Don't Kill for me.
Listen to the People.
The Emperor Has no Clothes.
We're in Deep Shit when
Bombs are Smarter than the President.
Read my lips: No New War.

What part of Thou Shalt not Kill
Don't you get?
Blessed are the Peacemakers.
Remove the Causes of War.
U.S. Empire—Not my American Dream.
Peace is Patriotic.

Drumming starts; marchers make room for dancers,
A helicopter hangs in the clouds.
Police on horses watch the centipede
Turn onto Seventeenth Street,
A woman as Uncle Sam struts by on stilts,
A small boy wears a skeleton costume,
A truck appears with a loudspeaker.
Chanting begins—
"No blood for oil."

The signs march on.
Drop Bush not Bombs.
The World Would Be a Safer Place
Without Trigger-Happy Cowboys.
Drunk Frat Boy Drives Country
Into a Ditch—
Starts War as Cover–Up.
A Weapon of Mass Distraction.
The Emperor Has no Brains.
Traitor/Deserter/Crook/Rich Man's Poodle.
Money for Jobs not War.
Regime Change Begins at Home.
Listen up, Cowboy: Real Men Wait.
Bush and Cheney: You Have Despised the Poor.
Money for War
Little for Poor
Money for Greed
Little for Need
Axis of Evil
Bush/Cheney/Rice
Johnson/Vietnam. Bush/Iraq. Let's Learn.
Feed People
Shelter People

Do Not Bomb People
Bush: The Real Face of Terror
Terrorists Hide Behind Every Bush
Bush: Evil-Doer/White House Squatter
Thou shalt not Kill Nor Covet Thy Neighbor's Soil
Honor Wellstone
Speak Truth to Power

On a face of Bush, the words: Weapon of Mass Destruction.

On a drawing of a flag, the words: Please don't make this Ugly.

At Pennsylvania, cops hold clubs across their knees.
We pass the Executive Office Building.
On cue, the centipede roars.
Two large painted doves of peace are held aloft.
A huge metal pretzel is inscribed with the word "Truth."

Let the U.N. Work.
Attacking the Iraqis is the dumbest thing I ever heard of
The Madness of King George
Drop Bush on Baghdad
War will not "Embetter"
War Equals Failure
War Gives Bush an Iraqtion
Loyal American Voter for Peace

A large Korean band comes by with a sign: Americans Out of Korea.

More drummers, accompanied by marchers in skeleton masks. Banner announces: Central Kentucky Council for Peace and Justice.

Another for Cape Codders.

And another for Brooklyn Parents.

An American flag the size of three doors is held horizontally by bearers with the sign: Patriots for Peace.

Violence is the Problem, Not the Answer
Presbyterians for Peace

Wellstone—We'll Keep Working
No Blood for Dick
Stop Bush Cheney Aggression
This war will make us less safe
It's the economy, stupid
Weapons of Mass Destruction—I am scared
I got Peace on My Mind
If War is the Answer You're Asking the Wrong Questions
Bombs Can't Protect Us. Justice Might.

More Banners—Columbia University, Baptist Peace Fellowship, International Socialist Organization

Dancers hold up "Not in my Mutha Fuckin Name."

Drums pound and a block full of tumblers beats a sudden energy,

An enormous dragon puppet sways past, and a devil mask.

"Take off your clothes for peace," one sign says, but no one does.

This is a family crowd, white-haired, purple-haired, middle-aged, parents with children, kids,

And someone who's written: "Hookers for Weed."

Stop Iraqaphobia.
War makes Happy Puppies Cry
We are Not the Roman Empire
Graffiti the President
No World War III

Behind us, a father has been explaining everything to his daughter, including the story of the vote in Florida and the Supreme Court decision that put Bush in office. He hoists her on his shoulders as we pass Lafayette Park.

And another shout goes up. We finally peel off, Susie needs to get back to help Jenny, who has moved into a new house today, And Jenny has planned a surprise birthday party for Susie and George tonight.

I ride the metro, holding the secret of the birthday surprise, and pride in my sore hips and toes.

And in my right to march,
With the
Signs.

Put to Sleep

Published in *Oasis* literary magazine 2013

My granddaughter Jenny calls to tell me
the vet will put the dog to sleep
late that afternoon.

I say "granddaughter"—
and you think child—
but she's a woman, thirty-seven,
with four children and
two step-children,
whose first husband, John, died of cancer
ten years ago.

The forecast is for frost.
"We'll bury him in
the back yard," she says,
and adds we don't have to come
on such a cold night.
She doesn't say we are eighty-seven
and she worries
about our
frailty.

The dog's name is Cartman
after a character in South Park
who has big feet.
This Cartman is a golden retriever
and climbs on our knees
ignoring commands
to "get down!"
When we gather at the table
he helps himself to paper napkins in our laps,
chewing with a smile.

Jenny's youngest son—
child of her new marriage—
is two, and loves to curl against Cartman's
red–gold stomach, hearts beating
together,

just as his brother Jeremy did, when *he*
was a baby. His father died
when he was two.

We drive in the dark night.
The family waits for us.
Outside, the trees are black shadows.
Jenny's husband takes my arm
so I won't stumble
on the stone path.
We stand by the deep, narrow hole
where Cartman lies,
wrapped in a blanket.

Four generations are present—
my husband and myself,
our daughter and son-in-law (the children's
grandparents),
Jenny, her husband, and her children—
Jeremy huddled on a rock,
the hood of a too-large sweatshirt
hiding his tears,
His older brother crouched at the edge of
the hole, hugging his knees,
his big sister leaning against her grandmother, who
wraps her in her arms.

The two-year-old
is in the house
with his favorite
babysitter.
The lights from the house are all on,
shining behind our backs.

The cold cuts through my clothes.
My daughter says what a good, gentle dog
Cartman was,
and I think of the lines of a poem—
"Grow old along with me
the best is yet to be,
the last of life for which the first was made."

In high school, my English teacher assigned an essay
based on those lines. What did Browning mean,
I wondered, long ago, and chose a different verse
for that essay.

And then Jenny lifts a shovel and digs into the pile of earth
beside the grave,
not stopping till the hole is filled
and more than filled—
we watch as the dirt becomes a soft mound.
"It will settle when the rains begin,
in the Spring," her husband says.

We turn toward the house.
Jeremy stays on the rock
until his mother takes his hand and leads him in.
Later, she tells me
when they took Cartman to the vet
the other children sat outside
in the waiting room
but Jeremy insisted that he come in.
He let the dog's head rest on his lap
until he was asleep.
"One minute he was alive," he said,
"then he was dead."

Daffodils

Daffodils kiss
the melting snow,
sway to robins
convening on a lawn
littered
with winter
where a young tree blushes,
swooning—
aroused
by the first kiss
of spring.

On Turning 90

Another country.
When did
we cross?
No visible border
no visa required
no right of return.

Weather fickle
roads erratic—
veering downward
without warning.

Memory tricks us
loses a key
a thought
hides nouns
scrambles for cover—
"whatcha-ma-call-it"
"what's-his-name."

Time collapses.
Now is all—
hand in hand with Death
looming in fog.

I live in
clarity of minutes—
cardinal's flash
of crimson breast
bud on the vine
bite of wind
touch
of your tongue
and mine.

Webs

I share my bathroom
with a spider,
thin and long-legged.

We moved in a month ago,
both of us starting
a new life,
learning our way.

It's twelve months
Since my husband died.
We were married sixty years
learning each day
to weave our webs
together.

The spider's threads dissolve
as the shower pours.
Each time,
it stitches a new nest.
And then, the water
severs the threads
again.
Again, weaving begins.
Again, I watch.

One morning
the spider is gone.
No web
along the tile.
I search and see—
it's nestled here—
beyond the tub
but close enough
to feel the damp,
the pulsing heat—
just as I feel
a touch—

like spider's silk,
delicate and tough—
stirring the veins
of memory
on my wet
skin.

Short Stories

Miami Dragon

Daniel leaned his forehead against the cold of the window. Snowflakes patted the glass and melted into drops of water. Across the street Central Park was coated with whiteness. Snow hid rocks and pathways, covered the tops of bushes and the seats of swings, like icing on a cake.

"Let's go out," Daniel said to his sister, Rachel. She sat on the couch, hunched over a picture she was drawing. Rachel was older than he was; she'd have to say "yes" before they could leave the apartment and go down to the street.

"I'm busy," Rachel said. "I'm drawing."

"But I'm bored." Daniel slouched against the wall and let himself slide down and bump onto the floor. "I'm bored. I want to play outside in the snow."

"It's too cold." Rachel didn't look up from her drawing. "Anyway, Mom said not to go out till she comes back from work."

"We could tell Bubbe Elke where we're going."

"No, we can't. She's asleep."

Bubbe Elke, their grandmother, always took a nap in the afternoon, and the children were supposed to be quiet while she slept. On school days, Bubbe Elke gave them cookies and hot chocolate when they came home, told them stories she'd heard when she was a child in a village in Romania. But school was closed for the winter holidays and the children had been playing by themselves all afternoon. Games, crayons, toy soldiers, checkers, pieces from the monopoly set were strewn on the coffee table and living room rug.

Rachel yawned. She was bored, too. She thought of getting out her dolls to play house, but Daniel never knew how to play that game and did everything wrong. The next day and the next day and the next would be just as boring as this one, until Friday, New Year's Eve. Mom had said that they could stay up to welcome the new year—1932. They'd listen to the radio and hear the crowds yelling and cheering at Times Square, and Mom even agreed (after much pleading by Rachel) to buy noise-makers for them to blow at midnight.

Daniel snuggled close to his sister on the couch. "What are you drawing?"

"A picture," Rachel said.

"A picture of what?"

"None of your business." Rachel put her hands down on the paper so Daniel couldn't see. She knew she was being what Mom called mean, but she was bored, too, by the long day indoors, and tired of Daniel's constant questions. "You're a big pest. Go draw your own picture."

Daniel pulled at her fingers, trying to move Rachel's hand from the picture. "Show me, show me."

Rachel relented. She held the picture so that they could both look at it. "It's Miami," she said.

"What's Miami?"

"It's a place, stupid. It has palm trees—like these, see?"

"Palm trees?" Daniel held up the palm of one hand. "I didn't know a palm could grow on a tree." He began to laugh. "Do they have toe trees in Miami too?"

Rachel giggled. "Yes, and eyelash trees."

"And fingernail trees." Daniel opened his eyes wide and stuck his hands out in front of him, wiggling the ends of his fingers. He did a dance in front of his sister, making funny faces and pointing to his eyes and hands and feet as he sang: "Toe trees, fingernail trees, eyelash trees."

Rachel stopped laughing. She didn't want to talk about the picture anymore. She really didn't know anything about Miami. Not anything except one fact. Miami was where their father lived.

Daniel didn't know about that. Not yet.

Rachel huddled close to the drawing paper, coloring the palm trees a bright green. She remembered the night, a week ago, when her mother told her that her father had moved to Miami. "I wish I didn't have to tell you this," her mother said. Her face had a stern expression, with two lines between her eyes—lines that appeared when she was worried or angry. "You know how sometimes you fight with your friends, and then you make up? Well, mothers and fathers fight, too." Her mother seemed to be trying to swallow something that stuck in her throat. "And sometimes, they don't make up."

"Why not?" Rachel remembered asking.

"They just don't." Her mother rubbed her hand across her forehead. "That's what's happened," her mother said. She looked as if she were going to cry. "Daddy and I aren't going to live together anymore."

"You mean get a divorce?"

"Yes." Mom pressed her lips tight together. "Get a divorce."

Rachel knew a girl whose parents were divorced. She was shy and quiet and bit her nails. When the children chose teams for relay races she was the last to be picked. Would that happen to her?

The memory of the conversation with her mother felt heavy, like a slab of ice on Rachel's heart. She thought about it again and again, especially when she was in bed at night. She wanted to tell Daniel, but her mother had said she mustn't say anything about the divorce to Daniel, she must keep it a secret. "You're a big girl, you're almost ten," she told Rachel. "Daniel's just a baby. I'll tell him, but not yet."

Her mother had told her other secrets, secrets that made her feel specially chosen, important. Like the time they gave a surprise party for Bubbe Elke on her seventieth birthday and invited Rachel's aunts and uncles and cousins. Rachel hadn't let a single hint about the party slip out. She'd hidden in her room to draw a birthday card, a picture of the ship on which Rachel imagined her grandmother had come to this country from Romania. She'd kept the picture in her bureau drawer for an entire week, didn't even show it to Daniel until the day of the party.

But this secret felt different. The heaviness of it never went away. Sometimes she'd forget about it, and then the words "Daddy and I aren't going to live together any more" would loom in her mind and she felt lonely and afraid. She'd always thought that being older was something like getting an "A" in school—like being able to read books with chapters, to cross the street by herself, to stay up later than Daniel and listen to a special radio program. But now being older had given her the burden of a terrible secret, and she wished that she was the baby and didn't have to know what she knew.

Rachel stopped drawing and looked at her brother. He was standing at the window again. Did he guess the truth? Did he guess that their father lived in a place she'd never heard of before—Miami, Florida? Her teacher, Miss Andrews, pointed to Miami on a map in the classroom—right on the tip of the United States, almost in the ocean. Miss Andrews said that there was never any snow or ice in Miami, not even in the middle of winter. A world without snow or ice. A world so different from New York City, so far away that Rachel was afraid she might never see her father again.

A film of frost spread across the window. Daniel pressed one hand against the glass, creating a picture of the palm of his hand and his fingers. "Look," he said, turning toward Rachel. "I'm making a palm tree." He drew two lines leading down from the image of the hand. "See? That's the tree trunk."

Rachel went to the window. She pressed her hand next to Daniel's picture. "Let's make a whole forest," she said, printing her hand several times on the frosty windowpane.

"Yeah, a palm tree forest!" Daniel said happily. Their hands thumped hard against the glass as they tried to fill the space.

"Hey, wait a minute." Daniel scowled. "You spoiled the whole thing. You can't see my trees any more."

It was true. Their hands had wiped the window clean, as if someone had rubbed it with a rag.

"Now you can't see any of the trees," Daniel said. "It's all your fault."

"It is not."

"Yes, it is. You put your hands all over everything."

"Oh, stop being such a baby." Rachel put her mouth close to the window pane. "Look." She let out a big breath, and a pool of mist appeared on the glass. She used her finger to draw a picture of the sun, its rays fanning out. "It's not snowing in Miami," she said. "I asked Miss Andrews. The sun shines all the time. It's really hot."

"Let me," Daniel said. He copied the way Rachel had made mist appear with her breath, and traced a circle with his finger. "There," he said. "Two suns."

The doorbell rang—long and loud, as if the buzzer was making an important announcement. The children raced to the front door.

"Who is it?" Rachel called. She pulled the door open a crack and peeked out through the chain.

Mr. Finch, the mailman, stood in the hallway, his face red from the cold. Specks of frost glittered on his mustache, small puddles of melting snow formed along the edges of his boots. "Are Sir Daniel and Lady Rachel at home by any chance?" He called out in his deep voice. He had been calling them "Sir" and "Lady" ever since they could remember.

Rachel slipped the chain from its holder. In the open doorway she curtsied and Daniel bowed. "We're here," Rachel said.

"Package for you. Which one of you is going to sign—your lordship or your ladyship?"

"I will, I will." Rachel raised her hand, as if she were in her classroom, trying to get the teacher's attention. "He can't spell."

"I can so." Daniel's lips bunched in a pout.

The mailman held out a package, the size and shape of the pan Bubbe Elke used for baking walnut cake. Long ago, Rachel remembered a package he'd brought for Bubbe, a large lump of brown paper wrapped like a huge dumpling with heavy cord. It had come across the Atlantic from Romania, just like Bubbe herself. This time, the package was smooth, neat, its wrapping as sleek as silk. Rachel signed her name carefully, each letter rounded and clear, the way she wrote in penmanship lessons in school. She and Daniel had never received a package in the mail before. "Thank you, your ladyship," Mr. Finch said, bowing his head to them. "Now I'm back to brave the stormy elements." He waved as he climbed down the stairs.

Rachel peered at the writing on the wrapping paper. Her name and Daniel's were printed in large letters:

To: Miss Rachel Gershon and Master Daniel Gershon
195 West 178th Street
New York, New York.

Her eye traveled upwards to the corner of the package. An address was printed on a white label. She drew in her breath.

There was the name of a store, and the city from which the package was mailed: Miami, Florida.

"It's from Miami!" she shouted. "Miami! Miami!"

"Miami!" Daniel echoed.

He began to do his palm-toe-fingernail-eyelash dance. He screwed up his eyes, wiggled his fingers and waved his hands, hopped on one leg and kicked the air with the other. Rachel skipped up and down the hall, hugging the package tight against her chest.

"Sha, sha. So much noise! Vas is das?"

Bubbe Elka closed her bedroom door behind her. She hurried down the hallway toward the children, smoothing her hands on her long black skirt and tucking strands of white hair into the bun at the top of her head. Bubbe Elke had lived in the apartment with them since she came to America when Rachel was a little girl. She now spoke English pretty well, but she still talked often in Yiddish. Neither Rachel or Daniel could speak any Yiddish themselves, but they understood what their grandmother said, and loved the long stories she told about gigantic birds whose wings covered the sun, about fish that stood on their tails and gave advice to poor fishermen, about Elijah the Prophet who wore many disguises and could talk to all the animals.

Bubbe had heard the banging of hands on the window and the clatter of feet dancing in the hall. She put her arms around her grandchildren. "So much excitement," she said. "Has the Messiah come?"

"We got a package, Bubbe." Rachel's voice was squeaky with excitement. "From Miami!"

"From the palm trees," Daniel said.

"See—," Rachel pointed to the writing on the wrapping paper. "Miami, Florida."

She wished she could say out loud that Daddy lived in Florida and that was why the package was important. She imagined her father going to the post office in Florida, mailing his present to New York, to their apartment, to this very room. Maybe he knew it was snowing today, maybe he guessed that she and Daniel had to stay indoors all afternoon. Maybe he wanted to send them a part of Miami. Maybe he wanted to come, himself. For a moment the wish to tell Daniel what had happened was so strong she felt the secret bursting out of her mouth, like a circus acrobat shooting out of a cannon. But she had promised her mother. She licked her tongue across her lips.

Bubbe Elke didn't seem happy about the package. She pulled her glasses from her apron pocket and stared at the wrapping, the edges of her mouth turned down. She shook her head and made a clicking sound, the way she did when she heard bad news. "Yes," she said, finally. "You know how to read. It does say, 'Miami, Florida.'"

"Come on, let's open it!" Daniel reached out to grab the package.

"Wait a minute." Rachel tightened her grip. "Listen." A scratching noise, tiny, but distinct, came from inside the box.

"Is it a dog?" Daniel asked.

"A dog? Don't be stupid. A dog couldn't fit in such a little package." Rachel held the package above her head, too high for Daniel's grasp.

"No fair!" Daniel jumped, tried to bat the box out of his sister's hands. "Give it to me." Rachel ran into the living room, pulling hard on the string.

"Children, calm down." Bubbe Elke called out. "Be nice, Rachel, let Daniel help. The package is for both of you."

"Yeah." Daniel ran after Rachel. "Lemme have it."

"No. I'm gonna open it."

"No, me."

Inside the wrapping was a long wooden box with small holes along one side. The box jerked on Rachel's lap. It moved forward, then to one side, then took a little jump. Rachel felt a sudden pang of fright.

Daniel lunged forward. "Be careful!" Rachel tried to shove his hand away, but he pushed past her and knocked the box off her lap. It fell to the floor, flipping open.

"Now look what you did." Rachel glared at her brother. "You ruined everything."

"I did not."

Rachel gasped. Whatever-it-was had run away. They'd never get it to come out. "You scared him. He ran away and it's all your fault."

"No! It's not!"

"It is so, you dummy. You dumb baby!" Rachel felt meanness rise inside her, like a spark that had been burning all day, a spark she didn't want to put out. Her cheeks were hot, her eyes blazed, her hands wanted to hit her brother, pound his chest. Why should he be happy when she had to know the terrible secret about their mother and father fighting, not making up, getting a divorce?

"Baby! Baby!" She pushed her face close to Daniel's, her nose and mouth screwed into a fierce expression. "Daddy sent us a pet and you made it run away."

"Daddy?" Daniel's eyes opened wide. "It's not from Daddy. It's from Miami."

"You don't know anything, you baby. Daddy lives in Miami."

"You're a liar! He doesn't live there!"

"Does so." Rachel spoke directly into her brother's ear, saying each word slowly and distinctly. "Daddy. Lives. In. Miami."

Rachel pushed him down and leaned over him. "He lives in Miami. And he's not coming back. Mommy told me." She was making Daniel cry, but it was too late to stop. "You don't know anything."

"Daddy is so coming back. He is so. He's on a trip and he's coming home." Daniel wriggled out from under Rachel's body, sobbing. He leaned his head against Bubbe Elke's skirt.

"Rachel," Bubbe scolded. "You know that Mother said not to tell Daniel. What's the matter with you?"

Rachel didn't answer. She'd been wrong to let the secret fly out of her mouth, but she couldn't hold it in any longer. Now her grandmother was mad at her, and her mother would be furious. And the new whatever-it-was was stuck under the couch. She bit her lip; she didn't want to start crying too. On her knees, she squinted into the darkness under the flowered couch upholstery.

Two small glassy eyes, like yellow beads, stared into her own.

Daniel crouched beside her, wiping his eyes and nose with the back of his hand. A black nose poked forward, then pulled back. "Come on," Daniel said. " We won't hurt you."

The children sat back on their heels and watched an eight-inch alligator crawl out, wobbling from side to side on spindly legs. He lifted his head and opened his jaws. The inside of his mouth was pink.

"He's smiling!" Daniel clapped his hands. The alligator stopped moving, closed his eyes and put his head down. Pale stripes ran down his back, his skin looked wet, as if it had just been painted—like a wooden toy, a toy waiting to be wound up so that it could begin to move.

But he was alive, not a toy. And Rachel and Daniel had never seen a live alligator, just pictures of gigantic alligators crawling through swamps, like imaginary dinosaurs, in the National Geographic magazine. Daniel reached out to touch it.

"Careful!" Rachel snapped. "He's just a tiny baby."

Daniel sighed happily. "A baby dragon."

"Not a dragon." Rachel frowned at her brother. "An alligator."

"Dragons aren't real. There's no such thing. It's an alligator. Tell him, Bubbe."

Bubbe Elke pursed her lips. "Alligator, dragon. Dragon, alligator." She folded her arms across her chest. "As men lebt, der lebt men zikh alts," she said. It was a Yiddish saying, something the children had heard her repeat many times. It meant: "If you live long enough, you will live to see everything."

Bubbe shrugged. "I never thought I'd live to see an alligator-dragon in my house." She shook her head. "I never thought I'd live to see such a thing sent from a father to his children. What kind of pet is this to play with? He should be ashamed of himself."

"It's a good pet, Bubbe." Daniel looked up at his grandmother. "Nobody else has one."

Rachel wanted to pick up the alligator, but something held her hand back: a frightened feeling, like the way she'd felt about a green snake slithering through the grass in the park. But she didn't want to be frightened. She didn't want to agree with Bubbe that alligators weren't nice pets. Her father had sent it, he had wanted her to like it. And the alligator himself must be scared; he had traveled all the way from Florida in a box, and didn't know where he was. He must miss Miami, the palm trees, his mother.

She patted the creature's scaly back and held out her hand, palm up. The alligator's eyelids rolled open, sliding into his head. Bright yellow bead-eyes peered up at her again. Slowly, clumsily, the lizard crept onto her hand. His tail flicked back and forth, delicate toes pricked her skin. She began to giggle. "He tickles."

Bubbe picked up the wooden box that the alligator had been mailed in. "That's enough. It could have germs." She held the box open. "Put it back."

"An apartment is no place for an alligator to play." Bubbe shook her head. "We should send it back where it belongs."

"No!" Daniel's face puckered as if he were going to cry again. "We can't send him back. He's ours. I want to show him to Daddy when he comes home."

"I already told you. Daddy isn't coming—" Rachel started to say when Bubbe gave her a sharp look.

"Rachel. No more talking about that." Her face softened, she touched Rachel's shoulder. "Sometimes it's better to be silent. If there's a thorn in your heart, it doesn't help to hurt someone else. Chochmoh—shtilkeyt." The sound of her grandmother's Yiddish words, their rhythm, was like an old woolen blanket wrapped around her, quieting her. "Chochmoh—shtikoh." Silence is wisdom.

But Rachel was still angry. Why should she be the only one to know the truth? Why couldn't she make Daniel understand what she understood? It wasn't fair. Her grandmother was right, the anger was a thorn in her heart.

She looked down at the alligator. He crept off her hand onto her lap and turned his head toward Daniel, as if he wanted to make friends. A thought came to Rachel. Not quite a thought, more like the glimmer of a wish that grew out of stories her grandmother had told. In one of the stories a poor farmer gave his last bowl of soup to a beggar. The next morning, there was not only a big new pot of soup on the stove, but the farmer's little hut had turned into a beautiful house, with a bag of gold on the table. The beggar had actually been Elijah the Prophet in disguise, and he'd rewarded the farmer for his kindness and sacrifice.

Maybe something like that could happen to her. Maybe the alligator had his own hidden power to reward kindness and good deeds. Maybe if she and Daniel took good care of him, their father would come home. After all, if their father hadn't wanted them to be kind to the alligator, why would he have sent it to them? And if they were both good enough, that might persuade him that he belonged here, with them.

The alligator wiggled on her lap. Rachel turned toward her brother. "Do you want to play with him?"

Daniel took the alligator from Rachel's lap and placed him in the middle of the rug. The tiny creature twisted his head slowly from side to side, pushed up on his front legs, stretched his neck backwards and opened his mouth wide. Daniel's face glowed with pleasure. "Look—he's trying to roar. I told you he was a dragon."

Daniel curled his fingers into claws and let out as loud a roar as he could blow from his lungs. "Hear that?" He said to the alligator. "You'll be able to do that too, when you're big."

"Oh honestly, Daniel..." Rachel was about to tell her brother once more that dragons weren't real. But she stopped herself. If Daniel wanted to think that the alligator was a dragon, maybe that was part of the plan for changing Daddy's mind. Maybe that was part of taking good care of the alligator, of bringing good luck, of making the thorn that stuck in her heart go away.

"I guess he is a dragon," she said to Daniel. "Pretend." She looked straight into Daniel's eyes. "We're going to take care of him and we won't let anyone send him back." She put out her hand and Daniel shook it hard, just once, as if they had made a secret pact, one that was theirs alone.

Diagnosis

"Are you an airplane, honey?"

The woman in black slacks leaned toward Neil, teeth bared in a smile. Liz felt her shoulders stiffen as she braced herself for trouble. Should she start talking about the threat of an early snow, the miserable airline service these days, anything to divert this stranger's innocent overture to her son?

Neil had been spinning in the aisle, arms outstretched, ever since Liz found the seats at the airline gate. She had given herself far more than the hour needed to drive to Pittsburgh, not only to avoid hurrying Neil, but so she could find a spot as far as possible from the crush of the crowd. The effort was futile, of course. How could you avoid crowds at an airport? Ben might have helped if he'd come, but she'd said no, she was used to handling Neil. Besides, this was Ben's busy season. "Don't worry," she'd told her husband. "I can manage."

The row at the back of the waiting area had filled with impatient travelers. A man in a khaki raincoat tripped and caught his balance as he stepped around Neil. He glared at Liz. She looked away; her eyes could escape even if she couldn't.

It was pointless to try to stop Neil, not when he was caught in his wheeling. At least his golden-haired beauty deflected critical glances. Small, delicate, he looked younger than three. People forgave babies, even when they blamed mothers.

The woman beside Liz held out her hand, intent on attracting Neil's attention. A string of bracelets slid to her wrist, clinking.

"Would you like a gumdrop?"

When Neil ignored her, the woman turned toward Liz. "It's awful traveling with children, isn't it?" Her jet-black hair bled white at the center part. Oversized silver hoops dangled from her ears. "I don't envy you. My sister comes East with her kids and it's a mess. People don't understand how hard it is for children."

You want to be kind, Liz thought. And you are. It's just that it's harder than you think and I don't know what to say, how to respond to your kindness so that it will last until we board this flight.

"You're so right." Liz heard herself repeating the automatic response she so often gave to inquisitive passers-by at the mall, in the post office, or anywhere she went with Neil. She tried so hard to shield herself that she'd begun to hate leaving the house, made excuses not to take care of everyday chores.

The loudspeaker crackled. "We regret that flight number 329 departing for Baltimore is delayed until 7:45. Repeat, we regret..."

Liz pulled back the sleeve of her sweater, studied her watch as if it held answers to the doubts that lay numbly in her mind. She'd hoped to get to the motel early, make sure that Neil was rested before tomorrow's interviews at the hospital. She thought of calling Ben, but it was too risky to search for the phones with Neil in tow. If only she hadn't had to check Neil's stroller along with her baggage.

The woman in the next seat groaned. "It'll be midnight before I get home."

Neil's spinning stopped. He let out a high-pitched "EEEEE" and flung himself onto the orange carpet. His fingers, tightly clenched, clung to the pocket flashlight he carried everywhere, the toy (if you could call it that) he'd discovered when he was two and took to bed with him every night. Arms extended, his fist touched the shoe of the girl seated opposite Liz. The girl pulled her feet back against her tote bag. She twisted a strand of frizzed yellow hair, her expression bored, unperturbed. Liz wanted to hug her for her indifference.

The pediatrician had shown Liz an article that described a child who sounded like Neil. The writer stated that for "these children" the sounds and sights of daily life were magnified—every footfall a crash, every spoken word a shriek, every color a throbbing glare. The doctor recommended a room with no distractions, and Liz cleared the furniture out of the spare bedroom, the room she had hoped to use as a studio for her graphic designing. She'd dimmed the lights, and stayed there with her son as he turned the flashlight on and off, on and off, over and over and over. Without warning, Neil would moan and cover his ears or rush to the walls and claw at them. Terrified, she'd call out, try to comfort him, but a kind of insularity gathered around him, as if he couldn't hear.

One eye on her son—still spread-eagled on the airport carpet—Liz took a small spiral-bound notebook from her handbag. She'd been listing symptoms to describe to Dr. Haynes, the neurologist whose name the pediatrician had given them. "Acts as if he's deaf," she scribbled. Ever since they'd heard about Dr. Haynes and his diagnostic center in Baltimore, Liz felt calmer. She dreamed that their real son was locked within Neil's anarchy, waiting to be liberated by the famous doctor's touch. Ben wanted to consult a specialist closer to home, but Liz, an Easterner, felt the rightness of this choice at the center of her being.

She reviewed her notebook. "Flaps his hands when excited," she'd written. "Fascinated by shining objects, twirls them for hours. Has hysterics if routine is changed." This last could turn the trip into a nightmare. Liz had packed the few special things he was obsessed with—a top that spun into a whirl of silver, a blue plastic ball, a small mirror. Thank God she'd remembered extra batteries for the flashlight.

Hot gusts of air flowed through the disheveled waiting area strewn with backpacks, carry-on duffles, styrofoam coffee cups, discarded newspapers. Neil still wore his red down jacket and wool cap, but she didn't dare try to remove them; the change might start a tantrum. His pale face shone with sweat, his damp curls lay flat at his ears. Liz kneeled and circled his shoulders firmly with one arm. "Come, sweetheart. You have to get up now."

The EEEEEE sound, scratchy, bird-like, whistled in his throat.

"You fell down, now it's time to get up."

The girl with yellow hair glanced at Neil and quickly averted her eyes. Liz recognized the reflex—the sudden awareness of Neil's strangeness, the involuntary pull away. She stroked Neil's forehead.

"You fell down, that's right." She drew him toward her seat, gently removed the cap. He held himself stiff against her body, not cuddling, but accepting her as she might the back of a chair. "Sometimes I think he sees me as a piece of furniture," she'd told Ben. Ben's face had gone slack, stricken, then hardened, as if she had accused him of causing the emptiness in Neil. She wasn't sure she could bring herself to make that observation to anyone else, not even Dr. Haynes.

With her arms wrapped around Neil's bulky jacket, she began to sway slowly from side to side.

"Sweet," the woman beside her murmured. "A gorgeous child. Are you from Baltimore?"

"No, Mercerville. About fifty miles from here."

"I hope you brought some lighter clothes. The weather's milder in Baltimore. Have you family there?"

"No. Not there."

"Oh." The woman held her hand to her cheek. "And you're alone."

Liz heard the query in her voice. "My husband is a printer. He's swamped with orders before Thanksgiving. I can manage."

The woman gazed at Neil. "Bless his dear little heart. I hope it's something he'll outgrow. Children do, you know." Her wrist jangled again as she reached into her jacket pocket. She plucked a green gumdrop from a paper bag and held it toward Neil's face. "Sweets for the sweet." The silver hoops at her ears flashed as the woman bobbed her head. Alarmed, Liz tightened her arms on Neil's torso.

But she couldn't stop him. Neil pushed away the woman's hand and lunged forward, his fist tight on one of the earrings.

"Stop, you're hurting." The woman batted at Neil's hand. Liz uncurled his fingers from their grip and tried to pin his arms at his sides, but he wriggled out of her grasp and ran, hands flapping in their jerky, frenzied way.

Liz swung her travel bag over her shoulder, grabbed her parka, her eyes on the red jacket as it wove wildly between rows.

"I'm sorry," she said to the woman, who shrank against her seat, one hand cupped at her ear.

He wouldn't go far. She'd find him, probably curled up in a corner with his eyes shut tight. She'd look for another place to sit, away from stares.

The hospital social worker, Ms. Rosen, smiled sympathetically from behind her cluttered desk. "When you first thought something was wrong, when was that?"

She looks my age, Liz thought. Younger. Liz wanted her to be old, motherly. It made her uncomfortable to answer questions posed by someone probably fresh out of graduate school. She scanned the beige walls of the office, not much more than a cubicle. A series of children's paintings—a sunflower, a boat, smiling stick-figures—were tacked to a bulletin board that also held announcements of hospital seminars on child development. Did Ms. Rosen have a child of her own? Did she know what it was to have a child like Neil?

Liz had been separated from her son this morning, right after their arrival at the hospital. A nurse explained that Dr. Haynes and members of his diagnostic team would spend the day testing and observing Neil. Tomorrow, Dr. Haynes would discuss their findings with her. Neil was silent when she left him with the nurse but later, while she waited for the social worker, Liz thought she'd heard his shrill screams behind the walls.

Ms. Rosen tilted her head. Liz tried to remember her question.

The social worker smiled again. "Can you recall when Neil first seemed different from other children his age?" She prodded.

When? Liz thought of the cradle she and Ben found in a yard sale, the weeks Ben had spent sanding, oiling the wood to its rich sheen, the tiny pillow she'd embroidered, and Neil lying on it, his hair fair and curly, even then. She'd rocked the cradle hour after hour, or struggled to soothe him while he stiffened in her arms. It had taken a long time for her suspicions to turn into worries, and then to believe the worries made sense. "I don't remember any specific time, any one thing. He was a beautiful baby. But he cried a lot. We had no other baby to compare him to."

"Anything else?"

The social worker wore a peacock blue blazer, her reddish hair fell, straight, to her earlobes. Liz felt dowdy in her jeans and turtleneck, diminished by the questions and probing gaze. She had an impulse to change the subject, apologize, bolt from this bleak box of a room. She was wasting Ms. Rosen's time. Nothing was really wrong with Neil, nothing that time wouldn't heal. "We've probably been exaggerating everything. Neither of us had siblings. We didn't know what to expect."

Ms. Rosen clasped her hands loosely. Her nails were pearl-colored, evenly rounded. "I know this is painful. I can't think of anything more difficult." She paused. "But the more you can tell us, the more we can help."

Liz let her breath out slowly. "When he was two, our friends' children were talking. Words, sentences. But we'd read that babies develop differently..." Her eyes strayed again to the paintings. "He was babbling. Not words. Not even bye-bye."

"And now? Is he talking?"

"No. Yes. Yes, he does. Not like other children, but we can understand him. And he knows words. The word for ball. And things he wants. Light, for instance."

"And his word for you? You and your husband?"

Liz looked at her lap. "He doesn't say those words." She bit her underlip. "Sometimes we think he doesn't know we're there. It's hard to describe."

By the time Neil was two-and-a-half, the pediatrician had been blunt about his concerns. She and Ben sat in his office holding hands as he ticked off possible conditions, all frightening—autism, severe retardation, schizophrenia. He spoke of inconclusive evidence, as if she and Ben were on trial. She'd felt besieged by the technical terms. They had nothing to do with the world she lived in, with the motherhood she'd imagined. That night, as she was putting Neil to bed, Ben lay down on the living room floor, one arm flung across his eyes. He stayed there till dawn while she roamed the house hugging herself for comfort.

The social worker leaned forward, looked directly at Liz's face. "This isn't your fault," she said. "It's no one's fault. Conditions like this just happen, we don't know why."

Liz felt the tears well up. Fault. The invisible flaw that fractured the earth's hard shell, broke a child's brain. Her apparatus had failed, her uterus harbored the defect. At college dorm parties she'd consumed the gut-burning brew of grain alcohol and fruit juice that everyone was drinking. It seemed sweet, harmless as lemonade on a summer porch. She'd often drunk too much and sometimes passed out. And how many times had she accepted a joint, casually holding the smoke deep in her lungs? It all seemed innocent, benign. But of course her careless ignorance didn't absolve her. She had poisoned her blood of her own free will.

Liz pressed her palms against her face, tried to hear what Ms. Rosen was saying. "There are excellent schools, camps, wonderful teachers... And no one can say for sure, at Neil's age, how severe the problem may be. There's a continuum. We know of people with autism, for instance, who are talented and intelligent, who accomplish a great deal. Even those more severely disabled can learn more than we used to think. They can hold jobs, be useful."

Liz folded her hands, stared at the rough cuticles. Ms. Rosen was preparing her for the worst. The social worker already knew what Dr. Haynes' diagnosis would be. They were all so sure of themselves, these experts. None of them really understood Neil. They hadn't seen how sweet and docile he could be. He'd begun to play with blocks, he'd line them up from one end of the living room to another. He didn't need their expertise. They didn't recognize the beautiful self she'd seen when Neil was born.

Her voice was low. "Isn't it too soon to know? Ben and I—we've seen improvement. If we keep working with him, isn't it possible that he'll catch up?"

"It's not a question of catching up."

Liz waited for more, but the social worker was quiet for a moment. "It can help to talk to other parents who have been through this—this confusion. This grief." Her eyes focused on Liz. "There's a parent group in Pittsburgh. It may be a long drive, but it's worth it."

"I'm not a joiner."

"Take the address anyway. Remember, you don't have to do this all by yourself. You can let other people in." Ms. Rosen wrote on the back of her card. "They can make it easier to get on with your life."

Liz thought of herself following Neil through airports, streets, malls, through stifling air, calling his name. She saw herself in darkened rooms where Neil scratched the walls, heard her own voice singing in monotone, coaxing him out of his fortress. The social worker had no idea what she was talking about.

"This is my life," she answered.

Liz held her foot against the bar of the stroller as she guided it down the steps to the hospital parking lot. The wheels tilted and she righted them, scared by the momentary lapse of concentration that could have threatened her son's safety. Neil sank his weight into the canvas, inert, as if drained by the past two days. There was no point keeping the appointment with the doctor tomorrow. She already knew what he'd say. This wasn't a phase, something a pill could reverse. The social worker had made that clear.

Where was the car? Where had she left it? She squinted at the endless rows of automobiles, closed and empty, like her son. She'd rented the car so she wouldn't have to cope with the uncertainties of taxis, but now the simple task of locating it seemed insurmountable. She wanted to scream to someone that she was lost in a strange city with a strange, insoluble problem, bewildered, scared, and alone. She wiped her face, remembering that she'd copied down the license number on the back of an envelope and folded it into her pocket. The car was in a corner of the lot, not far from where she was standing.

She tried to focus on what to do next, where to go with Neil. Not back to the motel, to the sounds of toilets and TVs in other rooms, to the soiled walls, the glass doors that led to an empty deck. She couldn't call Ben. She felt too defeated to ask for comfort or to give it. On the phone last night their conversation had been stilted, each afraid to talk about the question that haunted them both.

The man at the motel desk had suggested she see the Baltimore harbor, as if sightseeing could interest her. The ride might restore her equilibrium. She strapped Neil's slack body into the car seat, pulled a map from the glove compartment.

She wound slowly through the city's labyrinth of neighborhoods. Drivers honked for her to speed up, but she ignored them. Houses, delis, hair salons, churches, red brick walls, white stoops—all seemed flat, like a child's cut-out. Maybe this was how Neil saw the world. Flat, without meaning. Stopped at a light, she noticed a young child on the sidewalk wearing a fringed jacket down to her knees. One hand held a bag of potato chips, and she lifted the other, waving at Neil. Liz forced herself to wave back for him.

A chilly wind swept up from the harbor. Birds tossed, flags snapped above a line of pavilions. Liz pushed at the hair whipping across her cheeks as she bent to open the stroller. She raised her head. The watery air washed over her. She wanted to hold her arms to the sky, release a cry from deep in her ribs, a guttural, primitive sound.

"We've run away, Neily." She strapped her son into the canvas seat. "We've escaped."

When did she last talk like that to Neil? She wanted to lift him up, dance with him along the stone banks. "We don't have to go back to that horrible hospital."

She kissed Neil's head and pushed the stroller toward a pier where a large black sailing vessel rocked in its berth, a ship obviously restored to an earlier glory. The wind subsided, but the air stayed cool, laced with thin traces of November sun. Gratefully, she breathed the mingled scents of water, of wooden piles, the warmth of the brick walkway.

A small crowd had gathered on the pier to watch a mime, his face masked in white paint. He was dressed in lunatic elegance—gray striped pants ending an inch above his ankles, a too-tight black-and-white checked jacket, a large derby with a yellow plume, buttoned gray gloves with holes at the tips.

"A mime, Neily," she whispered. "Look." She edged the stroller to the front of the audience.

Every mechanical gesture of the actor's arms and hands was perfect, doll-like. His eyes stared, glassy. He leaned at a forty-degree angle, head at an opposing angle, his limbs jerking from one wooden position to another. He crooked a finger in slow motion, beckoned to a little girl with wispy brown hair. His toy hand touched his cheek; he wanted a toy kiss. The little girl looked back at her mother, her mother nodded and the child stood on her toes to peck the doll-man's face. Suddenly, his head turned and he kissed the girl—a real kiss, not a toy—on the cheek. She covered her face with her hands and ran to her mother as the crowd laughed.

The mime turned toward Neil. He made a sign indicating he had a surprise in his pocket. Liz shook her head hard. She tried to turn the stroller away but it was impossible to move in the crowd. The mime repeated his invitation, took two puppet steps closer to Neil, pointed again to his pocket. Some of the older children started a chant. "Candy! Candy!" Slowly, the mime pulled out an oversized lollipop and waved it in front of Neil's blank face. The chanting grew louder as the actor pulled back, pointed a robot finger at Neil and turned his hand in the unmistakable circular gesture for crazy.

Laughter rippled through the audience. Liz forced the people behind her to open ranks and let her through. The sky had darkened, a light drizzle began. She passed the black hulk of the ship, read the gold letters spelling its name. The Constellation. Stars. She felt fate must be against her. Everything in the day led to a dead end.

Perhaps she'd over-reacted to the mime, seen as cruelty what was only a vaudevillian's joke. She had hoped for relief, but her hope had tricked her, thrown her back into despair.

As soon as they entered the motel room, Neil began to scream.

"Neil!"

She pulled him to her and hugged him as he thrashed in her arms. She tried to distract him by blinking the flashlight, but he grabbed it and hurled it at the wall.

"Neil! Neily!" His flailing knocked her off balance. She clung to him as they rolled across the rug, barely missing a chair, and lay side by side, her hold so tight she was afraid she might hurt him.

He stopped struggling, but the screams continued, unmodulated, like an odd form of speech. She rocked him, her only way of answering what he might be saying, until finally the tempest receded and he slept.

Guests in other rooms must imagine she'd beaten him. She watched his face, her arms still wound around his body. Something had beaten him, something deep in his being, but his lowered eyelids, soft cheeks and parted lips offered no clue.

The drizzle had turned to rain. Liz listened to it wash over the panels of the sliding doors. The darkened glass repeated the objects in the room—chipped bureau, a lamp, a straight-backed chair, her body and Neil's, locked together. No one could help him. Not herself, not Ben, not camps and schools, not doctors. The social worker had said it: There was no way he would change.

She should carry him to his bed, but she was too exhausted to move. And it might be too soon. He might wake and start screaming again. Despite the cramping in her limbs, she fought to keep her eyes open.

Slowly, carefully, she withdrew her arms. She felt light, and moved across the room, floating in a trance, pulled like a magnet toward her bed. The pillow reached out, promising sleep. She expected it to be soft, but it was hard and heavy as a rock. She pressed it against her chest and stumbled back to Neil. Tears streaming, she held the pillow over his face, bearing down with all her strength.

She awoke immediately, choking.

Neil lay asleep beside her on the rug. Her mind, still partly in the dream, needed proof that the horror wasn't real. She thought of holding a mirror to Neil's lips in the ancient test for life. She bent close and listened to his breath, shallow and even. How could she have wanted to do something so terrible, even in a dream? She carried Neil to the bed, sat looking at his face. Her body shook.

Even with the lights out, the room was too bright. Car headlights flashed against the drenched glass, like moonbeams on water. She opened the door and stepped onto the deck. Rain splashed her ankles, and through the downpour she reached to grip the iron railing. She let her head hang back, let rain pummel her face and run down her neck.

Neil was alive. She was alive. She had tried to draw a ring around them so tight there was no room for anyone else, so tight it might have killed them both. Neil was what he was, real as cold water on her skin. Whatever she'd done or hadn't done, wanted or hadn't wanted, given or hadn't given, she had to forgive herself so that they both could live.

What had the social worker said? "You can let other people in." She had been alone in dealing with her son, as he was alone inside his frightening world.

Back in the room, she placed a blanket over Neil and wrapped another blanket around her shoulders. Her teeth chattered as she picked up the phone, carried it to a corner of the room where her voice wouldn't disturb Neil. She would not wait to call Ben, she had waited too often before. She wanted to let him know that whatever Dr. Haynes told her tomorrow—she would go, she could no longer postpone the truth—they would find a way, together, to hear the words, parse the meaning as well as they could, and decide what to do.

She punched the numbers, listened to the swirl of rain on the glass doors, the hum of lines connecting.

Paradise Garden

Published in *Oasis* literary magazine 2007

Look as if you recognize faces, Philip told himself—as if you expect to meet someone. He scanned the crowded lobby, batting the rolled-up conference program against his leg. Joss had coached him, early in their marriage; she was the one with the social genes. But she wasn't here, and he was out of practice. Besides, who could he recognize? The old-timers were gone.

He adjusted the name tag clipped to his lapel, with its purple ribbon reading Past President. The word "Presenter" was written in gold on another ribbon, a green one. He touched the slight bulge at his pocket formed by a stack of three-by-five cards—his speech, laboriously composed in neat, minuscule print. Plenty of time to go over it.

Joss should have come. It was an honor, after all, to be asked not only to speak, but to keynote a major session. The invitation had surprised him—he'd been out of things for so long. For weeks he was obsessed, waking up with ideas, spending afternoons appraising his choice of words. Even on the plane yesterday he'd scratched out phrases that sounded trite.

Joss knew he needed her here, needed her empathy and irreverence. It wouldn't have fazed her that just about everyone was young enough to be their child. She liked young people, felt enlivened by their knack for confrontation. But another bank managers' convention? "I'd just be in your way," she'd said. At least she didn't add what she'd told him twenty years ago, "They make me puke." She hadn't meant him or any of them as individuals, she said. Just the way they behaved in a group. She suggested they adopt a coat of arms: Egos Rampant.

He glanced at a nearby group of men deep in conversation, dressed in the uniform of the hour: pastel knit shirts and tan crease-resistant slacks. Phil paid no attention to the literature urging casual clothing that "catches the spirit of Florida's gulf coast." Joss teased that even at the beach he preferred jacket and tie. But now, he regretted that his business attire accentuated the distance between himself and his colleagues.

The conversation group was breaking up. He moved closer; one of the men looked familiar. Mitch Newcome, wasn't it? Heavier in the jaw, tanner, but who else had that tooth-gleaming smile, that way of bending close as if his remarks were a prized confidence? Was he wearing a toupee? His hair, still thick, lay in a solid mound—nothing like the billowing meringue that used to be his trademark. Phil ran his hand over the fringe of silver at his temple; his own hair had thinned and gone gray years ago. Back when he was president and Mitch one of the young Turks, they'd had a run-in about something—what?

"Hey, Mitch. Great to see you." Phil held out his hand, catching the split-second blankness on Mitch's face and his covert glance at Phil's name tag.

"Phil Mackey! How you doing?" Mitch grabbed Phil's upper arm. "Haven't seen you in ages. Where've you been keeping yourself?"

"I'm retired, you know. Haven't made the conferences lately."

"Right, right. How's retirement treating you?"

"Good, great. I've been consulting, keeps me out of trouble. Busier than when I was working, actually. Can't seem to find time to do everything." Just as well that Joss wasn't listening to this distortion. He thought about the long hours after lunch, flipping through journals, scanning emails, waiting for Joss herself to get back from work. "You are what you imagine yourself to be," a self-styled guru had announced at one of the touchy-feely workshops the National Bankers Association once sponsored. Pure drivel, those programs. Still, the harmless deception was somehow fortifying.

"You're looking great." Mitch grazed Phil's shoulder with a light punch.

Phil sucked in his stomach. "My wife is after me to exercise, but—"

"She here with you?"

"Joss? No. Our daughter's expecting. She thought she'd better stick around." That, at least, was Joss's rationalization, or his. True, Deidra, their only offspring, was pregnant, but the baby wasn't due for almost a month. "Our first grandchild," he said.

Mitch's eyes roved past Phil's head. Sounds—chattering voices, shrieks of laughter—seemed amplified. Phil cast for a way to keep the conversation going.

"I'll be speaking at the afternoon session tomorrow." He nodded his head, as if to answer a question. "On community reinvestment. I think you'd be interested."

"Oh, yes." Mitch pointed to the copy of the conference program he held in one hand. "I saw that. A hefty topic."

Hefty? Too big for someone like him, someone no longer in the game, whose synapses didn't spark the way they used to? Maybe Mitch himself had wanted to be asked to do it.

"You know what a hornet's nest those CRA regulations are..." Phil started to say. Mitch's eyes roved past Phil's shoulder. He extended his arm toward a tall woman in a purple pantsuit. "Hey, Glenna," he said, "like you to meet Phil Mackey." He turned to Phil, patting his shoulder. "Glenna Kleinman. The new Board member from my region, I'm sure you know."

Phil didn't know. He'd stopped paying attention to board elections. In his day, no women were on the board. With a pang of embarrassment, he suddenly remembered that he'd opposed opening seats to female members. That was the run-in he'd had with Mitch.

"Glad to meet you," Glenna Kleinman said. "What a coincidence. I'm going to be emceeing the session tomorrow." She held out her hand. Her fingernails—amazingly long, Phil thought—were a shade of lavender he associated with frostbite. Her hair startled him, too. Its ends seemed to have been chopped in irrational lengths, like one of those handmade straw brooms.

"I'll be introducing you."

Phil cleared his throat. "That is a coincidence."

"I'll need a bio. I mean I know who you are." Glenna tilted her head and smiled without showing her teeth, the way people did when they looked at babies or ailing relatives. "But I could use a few more details."

Phil shrugged, feeling his neck stiffen. "What would you like to know?"

"Maybe we could talk at the reception, find a corner somewhere?" Glenna pushed a stray hair behind her ear and smiled again.

"Sounds good," Phil managed to say. Surely someone closer to his own age, someone with more history, could have been picked to introduce him. He started to ask Glenna what time but she held her hand up and pulled a beeping cell phone from her purse. She touched the mouthpiece with her fingers. "Sorry. I need to take this. See you tonight?"

She waved to Mitch and Phil and ducked behind one of the potted palm trees lining the lobby walls.

Mitch was looking at his watch. "Great to see you. Let's have a drink later and catch up?"

"Right." Phil's gaze followed Mitch weaving through the crowd, shaking hands, delivering compliments and wisecracks. A politician at a picnic. That's what most success was, politics. He didn't have a natural touch; he'd taught himself to glad-hand, flatter, make small talk. Eventually, he got the hang of it. But he'd had to struggle, the way other guys in his high school classes struggled with calculus and trigonometry. He'd been goaded by ambition, his passion for perfection, the purity of logic that numbers offered. But his solitary childhood, growing up with only his morose, overworked father, hadn't included much talk. Certainly no politics or jokes.

With Joss's help, he'd shed his social stage fright. They'd met when he was a skinny graduate student at the University of Chicago, back from the ice-bound misery of Korea, getting an education his father would never have been able to afford. "This isn't combat, sweetheart," Joss laughed, when he'd complained about a party they were invited to.

For months he watched her stride across the campus with her friends, her brilliant hair swinging in a long braid. Expecting rejection, he delayed approaching her till almost the end of the semester. Later, he was startled to learn she'd been afraid he felt superior to her, a flighty girl from the North Shore. She left college and married him during her junior year, when he got his first bank job—a management internship in Washington, D.C. She took on the chore of entertaining the right people with light-hearted enthusiasm, while he assiduously remade himself in the image of a self-assured executive.

They were a team, or so he thought, until they weren't, not as far as his career was concerned. She'd simply gone and finished the coursework for her degree and gotten a job in a library. She stopped giving parties, stopped coming to conferences with him. A lot of other things had stopped too. He couldn't put his finger on them, but could still remember the vague pall of rebuke.

He was ravenous. He'd skipped breakfast, and these days his gut avenged unrequited hunger with sharp pains. The hotel offered meals in six restaurants, one of them, according to the conference program, "nestled in an exotic, not-to-be-missed setting, our magnificent Paradise Garden, an Eden of verdant tranquility." With such billing, he might at least get a good cup of coffee. He moved past clumps of chattering conference-goers toward a set of glass doors along one side of the lobby.

Glenna Kleinman had vanished from her perch behind the palm. No doubt joining a herd of look-alike upwardly bound professionals with cell phones glommed onto absurd hairdos. He'd drawn the line at cell phones, despite the urging of his wife and daughter, who both sang the praises of instant communication. "I can wait for news," he said. "Good and bad."

He rummaged in his jacket pocket for the snack the stewardess had handed out on yesterday's flight, and tossed a stale mixture into his mouth, grimacing at the saltiness. When Deidra was small he'd left snacks—bags of peanuts or M&Ms—on her pillow on nights he came home too late to see her. He'd tiptoe into the pink and white of her bedroom, guilt-ridden about his work-imposed absences. Occasionally on a free Sunday he'd take her to the playground. He had loved the trust of her soft hand in his, but he felt awkward squeezing himself into child-sized conversation, and helpless when Deidra disobeyed him. "She tries to get your attention by being naughty," Joss had said. "You're too preoccupied."

Joss, the interpreter of Deidra's world. He, the alien. The pattern had continued. A week or so before he left for Florida, his wife had tried to explain Deidra's state of mind. "She's terribly nervous," she'd said. "It's a big thing—having a baby at her age. She's 39, after all."

They were undressing for bed. "Why'd she have to wait so long? We didn't."

"We didn't?"

"That was different."

Joss began to brush her hair, soft gray-blond, worn carelessly to her shoulders, like a girl's. When they were first married, they'd lived in a cramped basement apartment with only intermittent hot water, and they didn't even consider starting a family. But then a year went by, and another and another, and when Phil started to get promotions Joss began to campaign for pregnancy. Phil's faith in caution ran deep; he insisted on greater security before they had a child. Finally when they agreed to try, it took another year before Joss conceived, and he remembered his anger at feeling that he was disappointing her. They agreed that they would have a big family, lots of children, but in the end, there was only Deidra.

The doors to the much vaunted Paradise Garden were taller and wider than they had appeared. He pushed through to an astonishing landscape, vast and peaceful in contrast with the claustrophobic jangle of the lobby.

Towering girders of steel and glass enclosed an enclave of trees and oversized shrubs with broad, polished leaves. High above the foliage, a waterfall cascaded over rocks and splashed on black outcroppings into a dark pool. A wooden bridge, draped with ivy, arched over the water. Beyond, Phil glimpsed stone steps—undoubtedly leading to the restaurant. But he no longer felt hungry. He turned to follow a path away from the waterfall toward more thickly planted greenery.

The musky aroma of mulch rose around him. He was no horticulturist, but he recognized oaks, dogwood, several varieties of palm. Every leaf, frond, flower, was groomed, signs of decay clipped away. Beds of purple blossoms clustered at the base of trees, hiding roots. There was an over-the-top perfection to the whole scene, he thought—nature in an enormous bottle.

He unbuttoned his coat. The air had gotten dense, humid. The path led through a tunnel of vines, crowding out the refracted light. Mossy clumps hung close to his face. He started to turn back, but changed his mind. He ducked under an outstretched branch and stumbled into a small, circular clearing.

A single sapling stood in the sun, its branches upturned in a bony pose. To one side, a brass plaque was fastened to a rock. Phil bent to examine the raised letters.

REBIRTH

In the early part of the twentieth century a rampaging blight destroyed millions of America's great chestnut trees—decimating the glorious forests that were once the pride of our country. The young tree in this plot of ground brings hope that those magnificent woodlands will be reborn. The tree comes from blight-resistant chestnuts found in remote mountains of China. When the sapling flowers, it will be crossed with a native American planting to create a new strain hardy enough to flourish again in our soil.

Carved into the margin of the plaque was a picture of a deer contrasted with the height of one of the ninety-foot giants in the vanished forest.

Phil was stunned that so sweeping a loss could have taken place without his knowing anything about it. How thin the sapling looked, what frail hope it offered. He stood riveted by thoughts of naturalists scaling Asian ravines, stuffing knapsacks with healthy nuts, then doing whatever you did to make a tree survive.

A metal pole held pamphlets about the American Chestnut. Phil took one, then two more, and shoved them into his jacket pocket. Deidra would be interested. He wondered if he should do something useful, like get water to sprinkle on the tree. Perhaps he should talk about the chestnut disaster tomorrow, weave it into his speech.

The thought jolted him. It was time for the opening session. He grabbed another pamphlet and hurried back toward the lobby.

The meeting was in a massive rectangular space the hotel called the Grand Ballroom. A room for all seasons, Phil reflected—at times a brightly lit state dining room, other times, like now, a flat map of chairs enclosed by walls that weren't even walls, but dividers, illusions. He felt light-headed, as if the walk in the garden had been an exhausting climb in thin air. The image of the chestnut sapling floated into his head. What would Joss make of his reaction? She commented often about his lack of interest in nature. "Flower-blind," she called him.

He chose a spot in the back and watched as people straggled in. It occurred to him that he'd sat in this room—or one exactly like it—every year of his working life. He imagined himself sitting here into eternity, meeting his Maker in such a room. He might even be there right now, already in his afterlife, his departed soul participating in a ritual of judgment.

Lights dimmed, spotlights beamed on Association officers mounting the platform. A drum roll, and another set of spots encircled the color guard. Philip half-listened to the greetings that followed, the droning summary of annual goals.

A few days before the trip, he'd taken Deidra to lunch at a small Indian restaurant near her office. She worked for a place with a name he could never remember, something like Friends of the Wild. The conversation had been full of pauses.

"You've got to get some other interests, Dad. Take an art course, I mean like life drawing. Painting." He stayed home too much, she said.

His daughter adjusted her bulk against the table. She was wearing a vast batik like a tablecloth Joss might have bought at a yard sale. "Do you know yet if it's a boy or a girl?" he asked.

"We like being surprised." Deidra pulled back her wiry mass of dark hair and twisted it somehow into a bushy ponytail. She looked no different from her twelve-year-old self; the same eager, pale face, the same clean, child-like nails bitten to the quick. The lunch had been an impulse. He'd been apprehensive, his wish for easy rapport made him feel like a shy suitor.

"Couscous pudding?" He offered from the dessert menu, much as he might have tried to please his daughter with Eskimo Pies on those long-ago forays to the park.

"Thanks, but no room." She patted her stomach.

"Your mother says you're working till the last minute."

"I take after you, didn't you know? I'm a workaholic. Thank heavens Mark is easygoing."

Easygoing. The good father type. Not like him. Not like the man who left M&Ms for his daughter and, when candy seemed insufficient, placed crisp dollar bills on her pillow.

His head snapped up. He'd dozed. Shards of light cut through the darkened room, crossing from one spot to another as names were called from the microphone. With each announcement a figure stood and waved. My God, Phil thought, they're introducing past presidents. Had he slept through his name?

One after another, balding ghosts, the men rose. Only two women had ever held the position of president and only one was here. When she stood, a row of females cheered. Phil could feel a collective male shudder. He concentrated on the year the woman president had held office. The list was going backwards; his name was still to come.

"Philip—" Even before his last name was announced, he sprang to his feet and waved, sat down before the spotlight reached his seat.

"Just a minute there," the master of ceremonies called out. He motioned for Phil to get up again, and Phil stood blinking into the glare. "You all may not have had a chance to read through tomorrow's program," the emcee said to the mass of heads that was now invisible to Phil. "When you do, you'll be delighted to see that Phil Mackey will keynote our morning session. Thanks for coming back, Phil. We're honored."

Pride shot through Phil's body. He clasped his hands over his head, mouthing the words "thank you, thank you." The applause seemed greater than the mandatory smattering that greeted other presidents. When he sat down his legs were trembling. He pulled a handkerchief from his pocket and blotted his face.

In the hall outside he thought of calling Joss. But what would he say? That he'd been introduced, applauded? That a few men had stopped to slap him on the back? People streamed out of the ballroom doors, groups knotted and dispersed. He walked briskly through the lobby, trying to look intent on a destination. He'd go back to his room, maybe rehearse his presentation.

He saw the blinking red light on the phone as soon as he opened the door. Joss came on the voicemail, her tone a pitch higher than normal. "The water broke. I'm in the hospital. You can call me there." Then, a heartbeat later, "Or come. There's a plane out at 5." He heard unidentifiable noises in the background. When she spoke again, Joss sounded farther away. "I have to go now—the doctor just came in, I want to hear what he's saying. I'll keep you posted…"

At first, he was confused about the water. Had the heater flooded again? No! She was telling him about Deidra. It had been so long since the vocabulary of birth had entered his brain. In his day, silences shrouded all that, though Joss had insisted on his being aware of everything, even tried to get permission for him to be with her during delivery. Nowadays whole families, even friends of families, crowded around the hospital bed, watching. What happened to privacy? Was Joss saying he should come see the baby be born?

He tried to remember exactly what date the baby was due. Joss sounded so worried. Call me, she'd said. But Phil couldn't remember what hospital Deidra had planned to go to. Had he been told? He ran over names of hospitals in Washington. Should he call them all? No, that's what people did in an accident. How bad was it for a baby to come a few weeks early?

He was accustomed to emergencies, making decisions. He'd call Deidra's husband's office. If Mark wasn't there, his secretary might have information. He started to dial, changed his mind. Better to talk to Joss first.

There was no response on her cell phone; she must have turned it off. He rang his home number, jiggling his foot as he waited through the taped message. At the tone, he blurted, "What's happening?" Joss had said: "Or come." How could he drop everything and come? He'd have to know more about the situation. Things could have changed by now, quieted down. There was no reason to be shaken up. Doctors knew what to do. "I'll be in my room—or page me," he said, and hung up.

The maid had been here since this morning. The room was pristine, neutral, reassuring. He'd planned to practice the speech; why not do it? But he was freezing. The thermostat had been set at arctic level. How could he work in this temperature? He switched off the air conditioner and reached into his pocket for his cards. Instead, he took out one of the crumpled pamphlets about chestnut trees. He began to read.

"...the disease began in 1904 and spread like wildfire... twenty to fifty miles per year..."

The thought hit him like a kick in the chest. The baby. His grandchild. Hurt. Damaged. Struggling to breathe. Doctors and nurses rushing through corridors to get there in time. He stopped the images. Nothing like that was happening.

Now the room was stifling. He threw his jacket on the bed, and his note cards scattered. He sat, composing himself. His speech could be read by someone else; the emcee would explain. He got out the airline ticket, fanned his face with it as he waited for his call to the airport to be answered by a human voice, not a computer. Yes, the voice said, there was a seat on the 5:00 out of Tampa. There would be a charge of $200 to change the reservation.

"Two hundred dollars?" He was aghast.

"Is this an emergency?"

"Of course it's a goddamned emergency. Why the hell else would I be changing my flight?"

"If you have a statement from a doctor..."

"Forget it." The fury went out of his voice. "I'll pay."

He glanced at his watch. Almost 3:30. It would be tight, but he could make it. The phone receiver still at his ear, he tried Joss's number again. No answer. Why hadn't she called back? He grabbed yesterday's worn clothes from the floor of the closet, stuffed them in the suitcase. He bent to pick up his speech, his fingers sticking as he put the cards in order. It was crazy to think anyone else would give this. Who could read his handwriting? He'd leave a message for the chairman at the front desk and call from the airport to explain. Maybe suggest that Mitch Newcome take his place. A groan rose in his throat.

He needed a shower, but not enough time. He pulled off his shirt and turned on the cold water at the bathroom sink, splashing his face and chest. "Clearing away psychic waste—" Deidra's words. Water was supposed to do that, wash away self-defeat. If only it was so simple.

He buttoned a clean shirt, stuck his arms into his jacket, listening for the phone. He closed the door, still straining from the hallway to hear the ring. Just go, he said to himself, wheeling the suitcase toward the bank of elevators.

The feeling he'd had at the opening session came back. He'd been in this hallway before. A million times. Same bland quiet. Same shaded lights along the walls. Same dirty dishes in a tray on the floor. Once, when Joss had come, they'd ordered breakfast from room service, and later put the used plates and cups by the door outside. The dishes were still there the next night. "Let's put a used condom on the tray, too," she giggled, "That'll get their attention." She'd worn a green silk sari to one of the conference banquets, long before revealing a bare midsection was a style. He caught the green of the dress in the wallpaper and remembered the fight they'd had.

She wanted to change things, shake them up. But most change was insidious, unseen. You could do everything right and never see the ruin under your eyes. Like the carpet he was walking on, hundreds of shoes wearing it out minute by minute. Like the infection that hit those trees. Like old age.

That's what his speech would be about. The first time I stood before this assembly I was a young man. Good opening line. He'd wing it, throw away his notes. Compare that time with today. Trace the incredible changes.

He punched the elevator button. There wasn't any speech. He could say good-bye to all that. There'd never be another chance. In the elevator mirror he saw he'd forgotten his tie. His face looked gaunt, his hair askew; he had toweled without combing. He was still wearing his conference badge. He started to pull it off but the pin stuck and the badge slid sideways. Why hadn't Joss called? Was Deidra all right? He closed his eyes. The young tree appeared behind his lids, its arms up.

The image persisted as he crossed the lobby to the desk to check out. His gut throbbed. He handed the clerk the note to the chairman that he'd managed to write in his room. "Everything okay?" the clerk asked. What an inane question. Did he know about the trees? The decimated forest spread in his lens—nothing but stumps and stone.

A woman with yellowish hair was coming toward him, waving. Who in God's name was she?

"Incredible timing!" the woman called. "Let's have a drink and talk—we'll get everything fixed up."

He held up both hands. "Are you crazy? It's impossible. They're all dead, for Chrissake."

"What?" Glenna stopped short, her mouth open.

Phil wiped his hand over his forehead. His mind froze, stumbled over explanations. The scene this morning returned–Glenna and the cell phone. "I'm sorry. Really, I—"

She backed away, her eyes scanning the room for rescue. "Wait," Phil said. "Could you—I mean, can I—" he gestured toward his ear.

"This?" She came no closer, but extended her phone.

He pressed the numbers awkwardly; his hand was shaking. One ring, two...

"Hello?"

"Joss—how's Dee?"

"Oh, Phil—she's wonderful. Wonderful. You won't believe. The doctor says this was the fastest delivery in the world—"

"Delivery?"

"It's a boy, darling. A big, adorable boy. I just tried to call—"

He couldn't speak. Then, "I'm catching the 5 o'clock plane."

"I'll be there."

He began to laugh. "Congratulations," he said to Glenna, who was still staring at him. "I mean, thank you." His laughter stopped abruptly. He handed her the phone. "My daughter just had a baby," he said.

"But tomorrow—you're the keynote—"

From where he stood, he could see the door of the airport bus open. The driver was beginning to shepherd passengers aboard. He reached into his pocket for his note cards. "Here," he said, shoving them into Glenna's hand and turning quickly so he didn't have to hear any questions.

He handed his luggage to the driver and slid into a seat. The vehicle jerked to a start, then rolled past malls and yards that could be anywhere, past a long pale stretch of water and sky. Staring into the window glass, Phil saw the hospital room where his daughter lay asleep, the infant cradled in her arms, eyes closed, tiny fists tight—yes, now he remembers the tiny, soft fists, the startle of hiccups, the press of a warm, sweet weight against his heart when he held an infant so long ago. He enters the room quietly, his heart almost breaking with tenderness for this new breath, this new curled, wrinkled being. And what shall he bring? What shall he leave on the pillow when he kneels to see them, his daughter and her child? What, this time?

    Nothing.

    At last, now, nothing at all.

www.ingramcontent.com/pod-product-compliance
Lightning Source LLC
Chambersburg PA
CBHW051438290426
44109CB00016B/1605